Brand Activism

This book critically examines how brands determine the visibility of social issues through their advertising practices, informing the ways we are persuaded to feel, think, and act as consumers and citizens.

Through a critical analysis of brand responses to ongoing geopolitical events, such as the Ukrainian conflict and the war in Gaza, Scalvini demonstrates how commercial objectives drive ethical stances, leading to the prioritization of certain profit-driven narratives and the exclusion of more politicized ones. Drawing on in-depth interviews with post-Millennial consumers across North America, Europe, and Asia, *Brand Activism* critiques brands' reluctance to engage with politically sensitive topics, particularly those affecting the Global South, arguing that this avoidance distorts the representation of moral responsibility in advertising. This book examines how 'ordinary' consumers—those not strongly aligned with activist consumption—negotiate the idea that they should take moral responsibility for their spending choices. However, it also discusses the rise of a new generation of consumer activists who reject superficial brand gestures and demand accountability for global justice. Case studies from brands such as Nike, Patagonia, Gillette, Dove, and Ben & Jerry's are explored in detail to unpack the symbolic, rhetorical, and discursive strategies by which present brand activist campaigns are being hollowed out and re-articulated into a moral discourse.

This is valuable and insightful reading for advanced students and researchers in Media and Communication, Sociology, Marketing, and Business disciplines.

Marco Scalvini is a Senior Lecturer in the Communications and Media Programme at the London College of Communication at the University of the Arts London, UK.

Routledge Critical Advertising Studies

Series Editor: Jonathan Hardy

Routledge Critical Advertising Studies tracks the profound changes that have taken place in the field of advertising. Presenting thought-provoking scholarship from both prominent scholars and emerging researchers, these groundbreaking short form publications cover cutting-edge research concerns and contemporary issues within the field. Titles in the series explore emerging trends, present detailed case studies and offer new assessments of topics such as branded content, economic surveillance, product placement, gender in marketing, and promotional screen media. Responding quickly to the latest developments in the field, the series is intellectually compelling, refreshingly open, provocative and action-oriented.

Branding Diversity
New Advertising and Cultural Strategies
Susie Khamis

Branded Entertainment in Korea
Hyunsun Yoon

African Luxury Branding
From Soft Power to Queer Futures
Mehita Iqani

Consumer Society and Ecological Crisis
Leslie M. Meier

Brand Activism
Advertising and the Ethics of Visibility
Marco Scalvini

For more information about this series, please visit: https://www.routledge.com/Routledge-Critical-Advertising-Studies/book-series/RCAS

Brand Activism

Advertising and the Ethics of Visibility

Marco Scalvini

Routledge
Taylor & Francis Group
LONDON AND NEW YORK

First published 2025
by Routledge
4 Park Square, Milton Park, Abingdon, Oxon OX14 4RN

and by Routledge
605 Third Avenue, New York, NY 10158

Routledge is an imprint of the Taylor & Francis Group, an informa business

British Library Cataloguing-in-Publication Data
A catalogue record for this book is available from the British Library

ISBN: 9780367616618 (hbk)
ISBN: 9780367616601 (pbk)
ISBN: 9781003105893 (ebk)

DOI: 10.4324/9781003105893

Typeset in Times New Roman
by codeMantra

Contents

Acknowledgments

I am deeply indebted to Sarah Fletcher for her exceptional research assistance and feedback, which have enriched this book. I am also deeply grateful to Lilie, Zo, and Monica for their encouragement throughout this process. Your belief in me has been a constant source of motivation.

I extend my sincere thanks to Professor Jonathan Hardy, the editor of Routledge's Critical Advertising Studies series. His guidance, support, and suggestions have been invaluable in realizing this book.

I would also like to express my appreciation to the anonymous reviewers of an earlier version of this manuscript. I am genuinely grateful for their thoughtful critiques and suggestions.

With deepest love and gratitude for their constant support, this book is dedicated to Marisa and Mario.

1 Media, Marketing, and Morality

The Ethics of Brand Activism in Public Discourse

This book moves beyond conventional critiques of brand power and marketing influence, interrogating the ways in which contemporary advertising is increasingly positioned as a vehicle for the moralization of consumption. Central to this examination is the concept of brand activism—a strategy where companies create socially oriented branded content that engages with social and political issues, often intentionally provoking controversy to generate attention and stimulate public discourse. While this strategy amplifies visibility for social causes, it paradoxically risks engendering moral inertia and consumer complacency. The often reductive, feel-good narratives promoted through brand activism can obscure the need for more engaged forms of social involvement.

By unpacking this tension, the book highlights the need for a study of both the intentions behind and the consequences of brand activism. This examination is crucial for understanding how brand-driven narratives shape societal values and influence the ethical frameworks within which corporate social responsibility (CSR) operates. Ultimately, the book offers an analysis of how brand activism, in its alignment with moral imperatives, affects consumer perceptions and reconfigures the broader discourse on social justice and ethical corporate practices.

In their communications and practices, brands articulate their ideas, concerns, or visions on various polarizing public issues (Kotler and Sarkar, 2017, 2018; Manfredi-Sánchez, 2019). This strategy is employed by advertisers to participate actively in public discourse (Sobande, 2019) with the aim of redefining which beliefs and values are deemed suitable for moral expression (Bhagwat et al., 2020; Sibai et al., 2021; Vredenburg et al., 2020). Examples of brands embracing this approach include Nike championing social equality, Patagonia advocating for environmental justice, and Starbucks providing a platform for transgender customers to express themselves. In this context, concepts such as 'equality,' 'justice' and 'freedom' are frequently invoked or insinuated to portray moral dialogue as an indispensable aspect of branding. Consequently, this transforms our everyday shopping experiences into a stage for engaging in ethical consumption, whereby purchasing decisions become intertwined with social and moral considerations.

DOI: 10.4324/9781003105893-1

Brand activism has grown in prominence as advertisers and marketers proactively engage with societal issues, incorporating social and environmental concerns into their campaigns (Accenture, 2021; Edelman, 2024; Mckinsey, 2021). These issues cover a broad spectrum, including LGBTQIA+ rights, anti-racism, environmental challenges, police violence, gun control, abortion, and responses to the Covid-19 pandemic (Bhagwat et al., 2020; Cammarotta et al., 2023; Sobande, 2023, 2024). Noteworthy examples of such campaigns include Nike's '*For Once, Don't Do It,*' supporting the Black Lives Matter movement (Nike, 2020), and Airbnb's "We Accept" initiative, advocating for immigrants and refugees (Airbnb, 2017). Evidently, brands known for their activism are taking significant steps to align their operations with their stated values. Ben & Jerry's (2023), for instance, has made a bold move by stopping their ice cream sales in the Occupied Palestinian Territory, and Starbucks (2018) has expanded its health insurance plans to cover gender-affirming surgery. These actions reflect a growing trend among brands not only to voice support for social causes but also to implement tangible changes in line with their public stances.

In advertising, marketing, and public relations, the practice of brand activism carries inherent risks and uncertainties (Bhagwat et al., 2020; Korschun, 2021). Without careful strategy and execution, it can lead to significant damage to a corporation's image and reputation and may even impact its financial standing (Cammarotta et al., 2023). A major risk lies in consumer backlash, often manifested as boycotts, particularly when a brand's activism is perceived as inauthentic (Vredenburg et al., 2020). Therefore, authenticity is crucial in brand activism (Banet-Weiser, 2012). It requires a consistent alignment between a brand's outward messaging and its internal corporate practices (Ahmad et al., 2024; Alexander, 2015; Edwards, 2010). This congruence between a brand's public proclamations and its actions is essential, as any discrepancy can breed skepticism and erode consumer trust.

Brand activism, while influential, also brings with it a series of ethical problems, primarily stemming from its performative approach to moral responsibility (Boltanski, 2005; Kazmi et al., 2016). This phenomenon unfolds within the broader context of global consumerism, where corporations craft narratives emphasizing care and social consciousness. Yet, these narratives are woven into the fabric of market dynamics, creating a scenario where the moral endeavor of 'doing good' is often linked with the economic goal of 'doing well.' In this setting, the essence of activism is frequently eclipsed by the allure of storytelling. Social issues become palatable stories that align seamlessly with the brand's image, potentially simplifying and commodifying social justice matters (Mukherjee and Banet-Weiser, 2012).

Examining brand activism more closely reveals a pertinent ethical challenge: the problem of selective exposure. Marketers frequently align brands with causes that are considered 'safe,' broadly appealing and likely to resonate with their consumer base. This selective approach is a strategic decision that carefully weighs the market benefits against the potential risks of alienating certain customer groups (Alexander, 2015, p. 17). While this tactic may be pragmatic from a business standpoint (Kotler and Lee, 2005), it raises ethical concerns (Banerjee, 2008). It often results in a fragmented and surface-level engagement with social justice issues (Mukherjee and Banet-Weiser, 2012); an engagement that prioritizes marketability over the genuine value of these causes (Powell, 2011). This leads to a situation wherein only the most 'marketable' social issues receive attention and support, while less popular or more contentious issues are neglected. This imbalance contributes to a distorted representation of moral responsibility (Drumwright and Murphy, 2004), where the depth of ethical reasoning are influenced more by public appeal than by the actual virtue of the arguments.

Another ethical problem in brand activism is the moral contradiction inherent in the tendency to adopt a narrative that skews toward moralizing (Hopkins, 2017, p. 128), particularly when promoting a positive outlook on social causes. This approach, predominantly centered on crafting feel-good stories, tends to frame corporate initiatives in an overly optimistic light (Zyglidopoulos et al., 2019). Such narratives emphasize the positive impacts of corporate actions on social and environmental issues, contributing to a perception of progress and heightened corporate responsibility (Carroll and Brown, 2018; Crane and Glozer, 2016). However, the focus on moralizing narratives in brand activism often obscures the structural foundations of the problems it seeks to address. By highlighting positive outcomes and promoting oversimplified solutions, brand activism can foster a reductive view that discourages a thorough analysis of the underlying systemic challenges (Scherer et al., 2013). This approach underscores a paradox: while brand activism effectively raises awareness and instills a sense of optimism, it simultaneously risks promoting a shallow engagement with social causes.

Brand activism functions within a mediated tension, as Uldam (2018) articulates, between selective exposure and strategic omission. These campaigns utilize media platforms to bring attention to specific social causes, yet this exposure is inherently guided by market-driven logics that prioritize content that aligns with corporate interests (Crane and Glozer, 2016). As Sobande (2024) argues, brand activism perpetuates a discourse that obscures the collective dimensions of social justice, replacing calls for transformative change with depoliticized acts of consumer participation. This selective visibility does more than bring issues to the surface; it reframes social struggles within the boundaries of brand narratives, often simplifying and depoliticizing them to fit corporate agendas. Consequently, visibility becomes a mechanism of control, where focusing on certain causes simultaneously obscures the structural inequalities and power dynamics that sustain them (Banerjee, 2008). Brand activism thus operates within a discursive economy where ethical engagement is commodified, transforming acts of social responsibility into gestures that may reinforce the very systems they claim to address.

The first case involves Gucci's response to climate activists vandalizing their Christmas tree, a situation that sparked significant debate. The second examines various brand responses to the Ukrainian War, showcasing the complexities of corporate engagement in geopolitical crises. The third examines brand responses to the Gaza-Israel conflict, an area marked by significant political and moral challenges. These examples underscore a critical issue inherent in brand activism: its tendency to foster a state of moral inaction wherein symbolic gestures of support risk supplanting more concrete, active involvement in addressing societal challenges. In examining these instances of brand activism, my objective is to unravel the layers of a paradoxical condition: how brand-driven initiatives, while effective in raising awareness and providing platforms for engagement, may simultaneously contribute to a more passive form of social involvement.

In the second section of this chapter, I outline the conceptual framework that forms the basis of my analysis. This framework is crucial for understanding the layers of brand activism. The third section explores the core purpose and motivations behind this book, offering insights into why this exploration is both timely and significant. Concluding this chapter, I provide a preview of the main arguments to be developed in the subsequent chapters. This overview gives readers a glimpse into the critical themes and in-depth discussions that constitute the foundation of this book, setting the stage for a comprehensive examination of brand activism, its ethical implications and its broader societal impact.

(In)action: Climate Activists Target Gucci's Christmas Tree

In the resplendent halls of Milan's Vittorio Emanuele II gallery, Christmas 2023 was marked by an extraordinary spectacle. A Christmas tree, conceptualized by Gucci, boldly defied convention and taste, igniting the displeasure of traditionalists (MilanoToday, 2023). Critiqued as ranging from unattractive to macabre, the tree became a nexus of discontent, symbolizing not the traditional joy of the season but the stark, commercial reality of postmodern society. Its drastic deviation from conventional holiday motifs mirrored a societal shift toward a fascination with commercial 'spectacle' over communal celebration. In a profound irony, it seemed Gucci was challenging the quintessential idea of Christmas cheer, presenting a tree that echoed a dystopian novel more than a holiday festivity. However, the debate took a dramatic turn when activists from *Ultima Generazione* [Last Generation], armed with buckets of orange paint, entered the scene (Buscaglia, 2023). Their intervention, straddling the boundary between protest and performance art, transformed the tree into a vivid statement, igniting a debate that extended beyond the tree itself to encompass broader themes of consumerism, tradition, and the role of activism in public discourse.

The activists' message was blunt: a call to reject luxury and advocate for climate reparations. The tree, now an unconventional canvas of protest, stood as a testament to their rejection of the extravagance and excess it originally symbolized. This scene, enough to dismay a capitalist and delight a satirist, turned a luxury brand's symbol of wealth into a vehicle for anti-consumerist expression. Then, in a twist laden with irony, Gucci chose to preserve the tree in its altered state, framing it as a "moment for collective reflection" (Salamone,

2024). This response was a masterstroke of branding. Gucci, a beacon of high fashion, adopted the role of a reflective sage, prompting us to contemplate the implications of its transformed tree. In this act, Gucci ingeniously turned a moment of contestation into a dialogue, a maneuver so adeptly postmodern it raised the question of whether the protest was part of their plan all along.

In an episode reminiscent of the 'theater of the absurd,' Gucci's decision to leave the tree in its paint-splattered state emerges as its most profound statement. This act of apparent non-action catapults the brand to the zenith of brand activism—doing nothing, yet framing it as a significant act. The audacity of such a move is staggering, transforming inaction into a profound action, silence into a declarative statement, and a vandalized tree into a symbol of 'collective reflection.' The irony is palpable, akin to the luxuriousness of Gucci's own products. This 'collective reflection' becomes a sophisticated euphemism for what is essentially a grand gesture of inaction. It's as though Gucci, in a display of nihilistic brilliance, has redefined the very essence of luxury—finding opulence in the act of contemplation and a sort of extravagance in the lack of action.

Here, we, the public, become an integral part of the Christmas spectacle, drawn into a collective reflection that seeks to convert superficial displays into deeper understanding. Gucci, with a cunning twist, mirrors this spectacle back onto the audience, thereby involving us in their narrative. This reversal of perspectives does not only underscore corporate ability to deflect but also elevates it to an art form. In a society fixated on action and reaction, Gucci's deliberate choice to embrace (in)action, to bask in intentional emptiness, presents a statement of almost philosophical proportions. It imparts a subtle lesson in contemporary branding—demonstrating that sometimes the most impactful action for a brand is a strategic choice to remain conspicuously inactive. While this approach is captivating within the realm of advertising, it also beckons a critical reflection on the ethics of moral action. It challenges us to consider the broader implications of silence and passivity in the face of significant societal and global issues.

This scenario invites us to critically question the role of moral action by influential brands like Gucci in normalizing and compartmentalizing political problems. As Bourne (2020) observes, the narratives constructed by brands are not neutral but are shaped by the economic systems they operate within, reflecting a selective engagement with issues that safeguard their corporate interests. What impact does moral action have on our collective ethical consciousness and our ability to address critical social problems effectively? At the intersection of ethics, aesthetics and politics in brand activism, we are compelled to consider how these campaigns influence public discourse and shape our collective understanding of social issues. Edwards (2018) emphasizes that public relations practices are not merely organizational tools but powerful influences on social and political life, affecting which narratives are amplified or marginalized. Yet, amid this interplay of luxury, protest and philosophical reflection, an essential question arises: Are we perilously overlooking the more pressing, real issues? In a society increasingly dominated by brand omnipresence, where a vandalized Christmas tree becomes a symbol for ideological battles, there is a danger that the fundamental crises—such as stark inequalities and ongoing environmental degradation—are being obscured by the din of advertising.

The Shadow of Complacency: Brand Heroism in Ukraine

The ongoing conflict in Ukraine, characterized by profound human suffering, has unexpectedly become a platform for corporate brand activism. In a show of solidarity, numerous brands have adorned themselves in Ukrainian flags, their actions resonating with the fervor of freedom fighters. Yet, these gestures are also deeply entwined with public relations strategies. This fusion of morality and marketing spawns a unique dynamic: support for Ukraine becomes a means to enhance brand image while ostensibly expressing humanitarian concern. The Western narrative's clear delineation of right and wrong oversimplifies the complex geopolitical realities, enabling brands to assume a stance that is straightforward and detached from the nuances of international politics. Such brand activism, opportunistic by nature, offers a position that is not only safe but potentially profitable, highlighting the marketability of solidarity in our consumer culture.

Take, for instance, Airbnb's initiative to house Ukrainian refugees (2022) and McDonald's provision of meals to those fleeing the conflict (2022). KFC has also joined in, repurposing its outlets to support Ukrainian soldiers and hospital staff (Business & Human Rights Resource Centre, 2023). These narratives paint fast-food giants and hospitality brands as unlikely heroes in war relief efforts. However, the irony, again, is palpable: corporations, often critiqued as contributors to global inequality, now emerge as saviors in a humanitarian crisis. This situation evokes an image of the Big Bad Wolf, infamous for its destructive actions, suddenly opening a shelter for the very victims of its past deeds. While these gestures are commendable, they represent only a minor part of a much larger and intricate geopolitical saga.

In the high fashion industry, brands like Chanel, Gucci and Balenciaga have suspended sales in Russia (Javed, 2022), a move that could be interpreted as a form of brand activism. However, this action, laden with moral implications, stands in stark contrast to their usual apathy toward other global injustices that remain under the radar of widespread media coverage. This selective approach to activism, as changeable as their fashion collections, suggests a transient and opportunistic stance, adopted only when it aligns with current trends and public sentiment. Such fluidity in corporate ethics in the realm of brand activism raises critical questions, particularly when solidarity seems as fleeting as the latest fashion trend.

Within the context of the Ukrainian conflict, the issue of moral complacency gains a heightened sense of urgency, particularly when examining how consumers interact with brands that stake a position regarding the war. In a strategic move, these brands tailor their corporate narratives to resonate with the prevailing social sentiment, seizing an opportunity to present themselves as socially conscious entities in tune with global concerns. This alignment often affords consumers a sense of participation or solidarity with the Ukrainian cause, achieved merely through brand associations or purchasing decisions. This phenomenon embodies moral complacency, where token gestures of support, facilitated by brand alignment, replace more substantive and impactful forms of aid for those directly affected by the conflict.

Therefore, it becomes imperative to scrutinize the genuineness of corporate empathy, a topic explored in depth in Chapter 2. This examination should focus on the ethical complexities of consumer interactions with brands during times of humanitarian crises. It raises critical questions about the true nature of corporate solidarity—whether it is a heartfelt response to human suffering or a calculated business strategy. Understanding this distinction is necessary in assessing the impact and sincerity of brand actions in response to global events. It also prompts consumers to reflect on their role and the potential consequences of their engagements with these brands, encouraging a move beyond superficial support to more meaningful contributions.

The dynamic between consumer perception and corporate strategy is a key facet of brand activism, highlighting a blurred line between genuine support and moral complacency. As explored in Chapter 3, this strategic approach of brands is becoming increasingly transparent to consumers, who are growing more skeptical of corporate motives. This skepticism often translates into a form of resistance. Consumers are now more inclined to critically evaluate the authenticity of corporate initiatives and are actively seeking more authentic ways to support social causes.

This shift in consumer attitude is marked by a reluctance to engage with brands perceived to be opportunistically aligning themselves with social causes without demonstrating an unfeigned and sustained commitment. As a result, these brands are facing a new set of challenges. They are now tasked with convincing an increasingly discerning public that their involvement in social issues is driven by heartfelt concern, rather than being a façade for self-interest. As explained in Chapter 4, this situation represents the present context of brand activism, wherein the intentions and actions of corporations are being scrutinized more intensely than ever before, compelling them to reassess their strategies and approaches to social engagement.

The Brand Battles in Gaza

While in the Ukrainian crisis numerous brands have adopted the national flag as a symbol of solidarity, in the Gaza conflict they seem reluctant to assume a position, despite the magnitude of the humanitarian crisis and the vast sympathy expressed among Generation Z for this cause. Ben & Jerry's has distinguished itself as one of the few brands to publicly advocate for a permanent ceasefire in Gaza (Speed, 2024). "It is stunning that millions are marching around the world but the corporate world has been silent," said the head of the board to the FT (Speed, 2024). However, this stance has not been reflected in any official communication on their website or in their marketing campaigns.

This move has reignited tensions with parent company Unilever over the ice cream maker's stance on Israeli policies[1] (Ben & Jerry's, 2023), potentially contributing to Unilever's recent announcement to divest the Ben & Jerry's division by 2025 (Karaian, 2024).

The contrast in brand activism approaches between the Ukraine and Gaza conflicts is strikingly evident. While brand activism in the case of Ukraine has been readily and easily adopted, engaging with the Gaza conflict presents as a risky and challenging endeavor for brands (Hale, 2023; Weissbrot, 2023). This selective engagement in brand activism, reminiscent of the transient trends in the fashion industry, starkly exposes the inconsistencies and fluctuating moral positions of corporations. Driven by market dynamics and swayed by public opinion, these actions reveal a fundamental irony within corporate ethics. They demonstrate a propensity for ethical stances to shift and change, reflecting the unpredictable and often fickle nature of societal attitudes and economic pressures. This dichotomy underscores the complex and often contradictory essence of CSR, where moral convictions are not only subject to ethical considerations but are also deeply intertwined with strategic business decisions.

Zara, ensnared in a controversy of its own making, offers a poignant example of the volatile intersection between brand image and global issues. An advertising campaign, originally conceived with no harmful intent, inadvertently becomes a symbol of war and conflict (Sachdeva, 2023; Jordan, 2023). Reacting swiftly, the brand retracts the campaign, a move perceived less as a gesture of sensitivity and more as a panicked surrender to public outcry. The hashtag #BoycottZara ricochets across social media, escalating from subdued online conversations to a loud, worldwide call for action. This surge in digital boycott calls exemplifies the profound influence of social media as a tool for connection, mobilization and ignition of public sentiment.

In an attempt to navigate out of this storm, Zara issues statements asserting its neutrality, a corporate stance akin to an admission of helplessness and a plea for innocence. However, this strategy of disengagement does little to quell the fervor of online activism. In today's digital era, a brand's narrative is subject to the whims and wills of a global digital audience. No longer is it solely in the hands of the brand's creators; it is continuously reshaped by a diverse and vocal online community. Each voice in this virtual chorus contributes to rewriting the brand's story, reflecting the dynamic and often unpredictable nature of brand perception in the age of digital media.

Zara's retreat, a concession to the court of public opinion, ironically begs the question: Why offer an apology for an offense not intentionally committed? In the convoluted world of brand activism, it appears that the mere suggestion of wrongdoing can trigger a vehement public backlash. The Zara incident serves as an example of the activist brand's dilemma—they are caught in a perpetual bind, with moral actions or inactions equally likely to draw criticism. Brands are continually navigating the precarious tightrope of public sentiment, where a single misjudged step can unleash a torrent of hash-tagged fury.

Activist consumers have called into question the ethical implications of these brands' global operations and associations (Lekakis, 2022). As a result, the same brands become the focal point of contention, often finding themselves at the receiving end of boycotts. In this context, the dichotomy of right and wrong becomes blurred, making the act of taking a stand complex and fraught with potential risks. For instance, McDonald's Israel's gesture of offering free meals to Israeli military personnel led to grassroots calls for boycotts, particularly from those critical of Israel's military actions in Gaza.

Similarly, Starbucks was thrust into controversy following a pro-Palestine tweet by their associated worker's union Starbucks Workers United (SWU) in the aftermath of a Hamas attack against Israel (Durbin, 2023). The coffee giant's subsequent lawsuit against SWU for trademark infringement exemplifies the dilemmas faced by multinational corporations in navigating the politicized use of their brand. These incidents reflect a broader trend where corporate actions, whether direct or indirect, can draw them into the vortex of political conflicts, prompting significant public and consumer responses.

The decision made by pro-Palestinian protesters, spanning from Sydney to Los Angeles, to target these brands is emblematic of a larger movement especially among younger people (Chughtai et al., 2023). It is not merely an isolated act of dissent; rather, it represents a collective stance against what is perceived as corporate involvement in the Gaza conflict. These activists, fueled by deep-seated grievances, have boycotted these brands, turning stores into significant sites of protest. In doing so, they challenge the presumed neutrality of these global brands, underlining the idea that such brands, owing to their widespread influence and presence, are unavoidably implicated in political dialogues.

The relationship and inherent contradictions between consumer activism and brand activism highlight a dynamic interaction between moral action and inaction, shedding light on the complexities of ethical engagement in the marketplace. Consumer activists often stand as the epitome of moral action, actively participating in campaigns, boycotts, and various forms of protest (Lekakis, 2022, p. 58). Their objective is to hold corporations accountable for their policies or stances on a range of issues. Motivated by ethical principles and a commitment to social justice, consumer activism is not just about voicing concerns but about effecting tangible change or eliciting specific responses from the brands in question. This form of activism embodies a proactive approach to ethical issues, contrasting with the more passive or reactive stances often associated with brand activism, which sometimes prioritizes corporate image over substantive ethical commitments.

Conversely, brand activism—or perhaps more accurately, brands engaging in activism—often exhibits a form of inaction that is cloaked as a moral stance. As discussed in Chapter 4, the involvement of brand managers in social or political issues tends to be superficial, driven more by the currents of market trends and public relations strategies than by an authentic commitment to the cause. This contrast, where consumer activists take a proactive approach based on ethical convictions while activist brands adopt a reactive and often strategically calculated posture, illuminates the complexity of navigating corporate ethics and consumer expectations.

This brings to the fore the need for a critical examination of consumer perception and brand activism, as investigated in Chapter 3. Understanding their motivations and impacts is essential to grasp their influence on shaping societal values and corporate behavior. While the primary drive of consumers is often a genuine desire for societal improvement, brand activism can sometimes align with these ethical goals. However, it frequently remains entangled with the underlying aim of enhancing brand image and market position. Recognizing this dynamic is essential for assessing the legitimacy of activist brands and evaluating their true impact on societal and ethical progress.

By critically examining brand activism from this angle, as is further explored in Chapter 4, we can uncover the ethical intricacies embedded in CSR initiatives. This scrutiny relates the inherent dangers of confusing consumerism with authentic activism, the distinction between which must be understood in order to develop a society that is not only more critically aware but also more actively engaged in meaningful social change. This perspective is crucial for developing a culture where consumer choices are informed by a clear awareness of the impact and limitations of brand-driven social activism, and where actions are motivated by a genuine commitment to addressing social challenges.

My Theoretical Toolkit

Scholars in both semiotics of branding (Floch et al., 2001; Marrone, 2007; Oswald, 2012, 2015) and marketing (Holt, 2012b; Keller, 2003) have increasingly observed brands as cultural and social processes that generate meaning through active engagement with customers and other stakeholders. Serazio's (2015) analysis suggests that successful businesses aim to facilitate consumer self-expression in ways that strategically benefit the brand while simultaneously acknowledging consumer autonomy and agency. Accordingly, Hardy (2021, p. 233) contends that critical scholarship should steer clear of oversimplifying and misrepresenting the media and advertising industry. Given the persistent interplay and evolution of the relationship between creativity and advertising, a discussion is essential for critique that transcends advertising's impact on supposedly 'passive' consumers.

The impact of advertising is often perceived as a threat to individual autonomy and dignity, a perspective rooted in the pro-effects viewpoint that posits viewers as passive and easily swayed, resulting in various social behaviors (Lazarsfeld and Merton, 1948; McQuail, 2010). Specifically, the pro-effects standpoint implies that advertising is the sole driver of such social behaviors. This viewpoint fails to take into account the active role that individuals play in interpreting and processing the information presented to them (Hall, 1997; Morley, 2003). By oversimplifying the relationship between advertising and human behavior, it may overlook the complexity of the interactions between individuals, their social contexts and the various factors that contribute to shaping their actions.

Marketers may dictate the content of advertisements, but they cannot control their reception (Eco, 1994). In many instances, viewers interpret and utilize advertising in ways that were not anticipated by the advertisers or marketers. Nevertheless, when these messages become embedded in broader political-economic structures (practices, systems, media, organizations, etc.), reinterpreting advertising in ways other than how advertisers intended can be challenging (Hall, 1973). This does not preclude, however, the possibility of viewers deliberately rejecting a promotional message (Fiske, 1987). In essence, while there are legitimate concerns regarding audience manipulation in advertising and marketing, it must be acknowledged that audiences' interpretation of signs and symbols is subjective yet formed by an array of social, cultural, and historical factors (Barthes, 1964). As such, the situation is not merely about marketers controlling the message, but rather involves a complex and dynamic process of meaning-making (Eco, 1976).

The relationship between advertising and media industries can give rise to creativity and value in promotional communication (Edwards et al., 2025; West and McAllister, 2023; Cronin, 2018), particularly through activist brand campaigns (Sobande, 2023, pp. 26–30, 2014). These campaigns possess a performative power that generates a conducive environment for social change and action, shaping the attitudes of the public (Bennett and Segerberg, 2012). Through distinct narratives, visuals, and discourse, activist brand communication engages audiences, garners support, and encourages ethical actions (Holt, 2012a, 2012b). Chapter 2 investigates the structure of these narratives, exploring how the portrayal of 'others' reflects brand positioning and its impact on emotional engagement with social issues.

On one hand, I recognize that digital media have encouraged a growing culture of participatory citizenship, encouraging individuals to engage in self-expression to support social causes. Consistent with Kozinets and Jenkins' (2022, p. 269) notion of "civic imagination," digital media platforms may be facilitating individuals in the visualization of a better future. To create positive change, it is imperative for individuals to perceive themselves as active participants in civic life and to contemplate their role within a larger community. They need to understand the process of social transformation and develop empathy and solidarity with individuals who hold differing experiences and perspectives. For those confronting the most pressing challenges, it is vital, at the very least, to envision a world where they are free, respected and afforded equal opportunities to participate in society, even if this reality has not yet been realized.

On the other hand, I am apprehensive that these new digital branding campaigns may also adversely affect the ethics of empathy toward others (Chapter 3). All forms of ethical solidarity involve a degree of egoistic 'altruism' or the inclination to benefit oneself through helping others (Chouliaraki, 2012). Activist brand campaigns differ from other marketing forms in that they place the pleasures and desires of the self at the core of moral action. This self-orientation leads to a contingent ethics which does not aim to engage reflexively with the political conditions that give rise to human vulnerability. The origins of brand activism, while partially due to the decline of politics in the public sphere, are rooted in more intricate factors.

These two opposing views make brand activism subject to two paradoxes. The **first** is the **paradox of complacency**. In contrast to the development of a moral character through disciplinary repression, as described by Foucault (1977), individuals in modern society are urged to perceive themselves as "achievement subjects" (Han, 2015, p. 49), continuously pursuing self-improvement and success. This quest for achievement is propelled by intense emotions (Illouz, 2007) and perpetuated through progress tracking enabled by digital media. While marketers undeniably benefit from this culture of achievement (Bauman, 2007), there is no external oppressor in today's society. Therefore, the contemporary consumer, characterized as the achievement subject, is no longer subject to external control but instead self-exploits under the pressure of an autonomous freedom that demands positive outcomes (Deuze, 2011). Viewing themselves as projects rather than subjects, individuals no longer differentiate between work and leisure (Sennett, 1998). In the end, the constant pressure to improve and optimize oneself takes a toll and is closely tied to the media that mold contemporary existence.

Han's critique (2018, p. 20) of present society underscores a significant consequence of complacency: the substitution of genuine diversity with self-exploitation and moral uniformity. This shift is primarily aimed at creating marketable differences, essentially commodifying the concept of diversity and packaging it as a part of social responsibility initiatives. In this transformed scenario, an individual's expression of social or ethical commitment, largely mediated through consumption, aligns with a neoliberal approach to self-exploitation. Han (2018, p. 19) describes this phenomenon as individuals acting as their own entrepreneurs, constantly engaged in self-production, performance, and presentation as marketable entities. This results in a cyclical logic where cultivating a self-image of social consciousness is intricately linked with the consumption of products branded as 'socially responsible.' Consequently, the achievement-oriented individual becomes both the consumer and the product—this dynamic exemplifies a key tension in contemporary brand activism: the pursuit of perceived social responsibility wrapped in the allure of individualism.

The paradox of complacency thus is marked by the contradiction between consumers' intention to contribute positively to societal causes and the reality of how their actions further their own inflated sense of self (Johnstone and Tan, 2015). On one hand, consumers engage with brands that promote social responsibility or activism, believing this aligns with their values and contributes to societal good. However, this engagement often serves more to enhance their personal brand or identity, a pursuit deeply ingrained by media narratives that emphasize achievement and success (Hollebeek et al., 2014). Chapter 3 demonstrates how the paradox emerges as consumers, seeking to assert their social consciousness, inadvertently fall into a cycle of complacency. Brand activism is thus adopted not primarily for the cause itself, but to fulfill internalized expectations of personal achievement and societal approval (Boyd et al., 2016).

The **second paradox** within the realm of brand activism is that of **'moral (in)action**.' As discussed in Chapters 2 and 4, this paradox posits that the representation of social causes in media and marketing campaigns may lead to selective empathy, counterintuitively inhibiting moral reasoning rather than stimulating it (Chouliaraki, 2006, 2013). Empathy, a driving force behind moral actions, allows us to understand and share the feelings of others, playing a crucial role in moral decision-making. However, as Bloom (2017) argues, empathy is not without its biases. As highlighted in Chapter 3, we are often more inclined to empathize with individuals who are similar to us or who share our values and beliefs, potentially leading to the unjust treatment or exclusion of those who differ from us in our moral considerations.

This becomes particularly problematic in brand activism, where social causes are often packaged and presented in ways that align with the brand's image and values, potentially leading to a selective and biased form of empathy. As examined in Chapter 2, this paradox reflects the dilemma of the 'mediated other,' a concept initially identified in the context of infotainment (Boltanski, 1999; Silverstone, 2002). The convergence of marketing and media through branded content exacerbates the issue of moral (in)action on a larger scale, highlighting an increasingly symbiotic relationship between media content and market forces (Habermas, 1989). This state of affairs suggests that moral action is often colored by commercial exchange logic, where assisting the vulnerable becomes subordinate to the capitalist principle of profit maximization (Fraser, 2023). This subordination of morality to market interests implies that mediated forms of empathy might encourage contemplative consumption of sensationalized content rather than spurring meaningful action.

The commodification of social issues in brand activism fosters a voyeuristic or 'pornographic' attitude toward empathy (Sontag, 2003), diminishing the urgency and reality of these situations and relegating them to the realm of fiction. While it is important to recognize that such brand strategies can certainly raise awareness of social causes, this awareness is often instrumental to the market agenda. This dynamic presents ethical challenges and prompts questions about the impact of brand strategies that exploit social issues for profitability. Such strategies have the potential to desensitize audiences and dilute their drive for genuine, real-world action and solidarity. In sum, while brand activism can spotlight important issues, it often does so in a way that aligns with and serves corporate marketing goals, potentially transforming urgent social causes into mere tools for brand promotion.

The paradox of moral (in)action underscores the complexities that emerge from the tension between our moral obligations and our capacity to fulfill them. Originating from Singer's (1972) discussions on ethical actions, this paradox often arises in scenarios where conflicting moral demands are present or where the morally 'right' course of action is either challenging or unachievable (Tessman, 2014). Our moral responsibilities are typically grounded in a sense of duty toward others and adherence to principles of justice and fairness (Rawls, 1971). This trend often contradicts the ideals of authentic self-expression and genuine connection with others (Taylor, 2018), leading to a scenario where ethical actions are compromised or overshadowed by consumerist behaviors and market dynamics.

The examination of moral (in)action and complacency, framed through Baudrillard's theory of the simulacrum (1983), challenges traditional notions of moral engagement. Baudrillard's concept suggests that the boundaries between genuine activism and passive complacency are increasingly blurred in a context where audiences often encounter social causes as simulations rather than direct experiences. This blurring complicates the ability to take effective action against social injustices, as the distinction between real issues and their mediated portrayals becomes increasingly difficult to discern. In a hyper-real society, as Baudrillard (1994) argues, simulations of moral action can sometimes substitute for actual efforts, suggesting that the appearance of action is prioritized over substantive engagement. This dynamic challenges our understanding of moral responsibility, urging a critical evaluation of how contemporary society interprets and responds to calls for action, particularly within the pervasive frameworks of advertising and media.

What This Book Is About

The book is structured with dual objectives guiding its analytical journey. The **first objective** involves a critical examination of the transmission and reception of moral values through advertising (Chapter 2). This examination dissects how advertising effectively conveys moral messages and scrutinizes how activist brand campaigns differentiate themselves from traditional corporate campaigns. This analysis aims to provide a comprehensive understanding of how these brand campaigns reflect and influence shifts in moralization strategies associated with brands. Moreover, it seeks to explore the broader implications of these shifts, particularly in terms of how they mirror and contribute to transformations in societal solidarity and the political landscape.

The **second objective** is to explore the ethical motivations and commitments underlying brand activism, from the perspectives of both consumers

(Chapters 3 and 4) and marketers (Chapter 4) respectively. This exploration seeks to understand how advertising not only conveys moral messages but also how these messages are interpreted by the public. It examines the degrees of how advertising shapes public discourse on ethical matters and the role of advertising in both reflecting and influencing societal values and norms. This dual approach aims to provide a comprehensive understanding of the complex interaction between brand messaging, consumer perception and the broader implications for ethical reasoning and social responsibility in the context of advertising.

In addressing the first objective of this book—critically analyzing the transmission and reception of moral values through advertising, as well as its influence on public discourse and ethical frameworks—a comparison between Chouliaraki's work (2006, 2013) and my research on brand activism is particularly valuable. Chouliaraki's critique of branding in humanitarian contexts, as detailed in *The Ironic Spectator* (2013), aids in examining how moral values are communicated and understood within brand-driven initiatives. This contribution provides also a foundation for understanding how advertising not only reflects but also actively mediates moral values. This perspective is essential for understanding that advertising does more than reflect existing moral frameworks; it actively redefines the ontology of moral space. However, advertising frequently intertwines ethical engagement with strategic self-interest, complicating its role in shaping moral discourse. This book examines how advertising shapes and distorts moral values, raising important questions about the ethical implications of brand activism in contemporary media culture.

To meet the second objective of this book—examining the ethical motivations and commitments underlying brand activism from both consumer and marketer perspectives—it is necessary to consider the foundational works of the early 21st century and the subsequent development of two distinct schools of thought. Klein's *No LOGO* (2000) and Hardt and Negri's *Empire* (2000) exposed the pervasive reach of advertising and its influence on global capitalist structures. This critique led to a debate that crystallized into two opposing viewpoints: the "anti-consumerism" perspective, which critiques the omnipresence of marketing and advocates for consumer restraint, and the "consumer-as-agent" perspective, which emphasizes consumer empowerment in the face of corporate branding (Mukherjee and Banet-Weiser, 2012, p. 11). These contrasting perspectives provide a critical framework for analyzing the ethical dimensions of brand activism.

The anti-consumerism stance raises concerns about the pervasive influence of advertising and its potential to manipulate consumer choices. Conversely, the consumer-as-agent viewpoint highlights the role of informed decision-making, challenging the perception of branding as purely a corporate tactic. My approach neither wholly condemns the advertising industry as manipulative nor overestimates consumer power. Instead, it recognizes the industry's role in both reflecting and shaping cultural and social changes. This approach offers a comprehensive understanding of the relationship between creativity, consumer choice, and ethical considerations in brand activism, providing insights into how these factors influence and shape the broader ethical dynamics within society.

This perspective directly engages with critiques such as Hardy's (2021), which caution against oversimplifying the media and advertising industry. By emphasizing the evolving and interconnected nature of these relationships, this approach calls for ongoing examination of how consumer moral actions are influenced by societal structures and cultural narratives. In this way, I recognize that consumers operate within specific societal structures and cultural narratives that shape their moral decisions. By analyzing these frameworks empirically, researchers can identify how societal norms influence consumer choices and how these choices, in turn, can reinforce or challenge existing moral standards. For these reasons, in this book, I adopted an empirically informed approach to ethics (Christen et al., 2016), highlighting the significance of normative frameworks that shape consumer behavior. This approach allows for the collection of data on how consumers actually behave in moral contexts. This data can reveal patterns of behavior that might not align with traditional ethical theories, thereby offering a more accurate picture of moral agency in consumer actions.

Despite the book's foundation in a series of in-depth interviews (Chapters 3 and 4), I intentionally move away from the neo-positivist approach that dominates much of social science research. This approach, which emphasizes empirical, observable, and quantifiable evidence as the primary basis for knowledge, is critically examined in my work. Drawing on Adorno's (1973, 2014) critique, I argue that such data analysis often reduces social phenomena to rigid categories, overlooking the rich qualitative, subjective, and often contradictory aspects of human experience and social reality. In the context of promotional communication (West and McAllister, 2023; Edwards et al., 2025), this reductionist perspective risks oversimplifying the relationships between individual motivations, societal values, and corporate strategies.

My approach, therefore, embraces a more interpretive and reflective analysis (Braun and Clarke, 2022), which recognizes the multiple layers of meaning, perception, and emotion embedded within the data. This analysis allows for an exploration of how individuals and groups experience brand activism, not just as a series of messages or actions, but as phenomena deeply intertwined with identity, ideology, and power. By applying this framework, the analysis can capture the complex ways in which promotional communication shapes and is shaped by broader social realities, offering a more comprehensive understanding of the ethical implications of the communicative strategies adopted in brand activist campaigns.

Therefore, this book implicitly critiques much of the existing media ethics analysis, recognizing that the ethical dimensions of brand activism are filled with contradictions and complexities that resist straightforward categorization. This specificity challenges the traditional binary understanding of ethical actions (wrong/right) and compels a more multifaceted examination. By avoiding the confinement of moral reasoning within rigid frameworks, the book enables a thorough examination of the ambiguities and dilemmas that characterize brand activism. It encourages a more holistic understanding of ethics, one that contemplates the diverse and sometimes conflicting dimensions of corporate actions, consumer agency and societal impact. Therefore, understanding the ethical dimensions of brand activism requires moving beyond surface-level judgments to engage with the broader moral implications at play.

The forthcoming chapters provide a set of analytical frameworks designed to interrogate the contradictions within brand activism.

The Structure of the Book

Building on the theoretical foundation laid in the first chapter, subsequent chapters explore the practical applications and implications of brand activism in today's world. Each chapter bridges theory and practice, moving from abstract concepts to empirical analysis of real-world brand activism campaigns. This approach not only demonstrates the relevance of normative theory in promotional communication but also invites readers to critically engage with the ethical complexities inherent to brand activism. Through dissecting and examining the narratives and strategies behind various campaigns, readers gain a comprehensive understanding of how brands articulate their activist messages, how these messages resonate with consumers, and the potential ethical implications of these interactions.

In Chapter 2, I present an array of brand activism campaigns, conducting a detailed content analysis of their themes, content, and underlying messages from 2018 to 2022. This analysis is aimed at uncovering the levels of moral engagement and competency required from consumers by these campaigns. My objective is to develop a taxonomy that categorizes various degrees of engagement with moral issues and the extent of moral competency demanded from viewers. This chapter also critically examines the tendency of brand campaigns to favor emotional appeal over substantive action. It emphasizes the importance of striking a careful balance between raising awareness and driving authentic change that extends beyond simple brand promotion.

A significant focus of this chapter is on the empathic portrayal of 'the Other' in these campaigns, particularly how vulnerable groups, often marginalized or oppressed, are represented. It highlights the ethical challenges involved in such portrayals—whether these narratives authentically amplify the voices of these groups or if they are overshadowed by the brand's marketing objectives.

Crafting empathic narratives responsibly is a substantial ethical burden for advertisers, requiring meticulous consideration of narrative construction, imagery, and rhetoric. Brands are tasked with creating narratives that are not just captivating but also ethically sound and respectful.

However, the resolution to these ethical challenges is not found in simply establishing rigid moral guidelines for advertisers. Instead, the chapter argues for the adoption of an analytical framework to critically assess the representation of the other. This taxonomy can be adopted to ensure that audience engagement with these narratives accurately reflects the realities of the groups represented and effectively contributes to significant social change. This approach necessitates a more discerning understanding of the role of brand activism in shaping public discourse and its implications for social justice.

In Chapter 3, I explore the broader implications of algorithmic recommendation systems on moral thinking and action, investigating whether digital platforms contribute to a decline in moral reflection as consumers become more focused on personal gratification than the wider consequences of their actions. I primarily address the theoretical discourse on advertising's role in cultivating empathy, advocating for a discerning view that acknowledges how individuals perceive empathetic representations. The chapter also addresses two research questions. The first question examines how the public engages with and interprets empathy-based representations in digital brand activism campaigns. This investigation is significant for understanding the impact of digital narratives on public perception and emotional response. The second question assesses the ethical responsibilities of marketers and advertisers in using empathetic representations in their campaigns.

Drawing on in-depth interviews, the chapter explores the contradictions that arise when empathy in advertising does not lead to moral action. This part of the analysis is crucial for evaluating the effectiveness of empathetic messaging in motivating ethical consumer behavior and for understanding the ethical challenges faced by advertisers in crafting these messages. Therefore, I argue for a dialogical approach in brand messaging, combining empathy with ethical clarity to motivate audiences toward actionable support for systemic change. The goal is for brand activism campaigns to go beyond performative gestures, contributing meaningfully to social justice.

Next, in Chapter 4, I critically examine the disconnect between the strategic framing of brand activism by managers and the affective engagement sought by young adult consumers, drawing on interviews with both groups. My analysis reveals a generational divide in the perception of brand activism: while brand managers often treat activism as a calculated strategic and moral performance, young adults—who are increasingly media-savvy and critically aware—demand greater transparency, tangible impact, and meaningful engagement. These consumers also grapple with the expectation that they must assume moral responsibility for their spending choices, negotiating the tension between ethical consumption and systemic limitations.

This gap highlights the need for brands to move beyond performative gestures and engage in activism that resonates within the cultural and ideological circuits of their audiences. I argue that effective brand activism requires a careful calibration of moral signaling and actionable outcomes, ensuring that it aligns with the broader cultural codes and discourses of justice that are meaningful to a critically aware public. In this context, the primary challenge is not merely to deploy empathy as a rhetorical device but to embed it within practices that catalyze substantive societal change.

In Chapter 5, I conclude by reexamining the ethical dilemmas inherent in brand activism, beginning with the issue of empathy when it is deployed from a position of privilege. This self-referential moral engagement often leads to campaigns prioritizing causes that align with marketable interests and resonate with a Western consumer base. As a result, more pressing ethical concerns, particularly those affecting the Global South, are neglected or oversimplified, distorting the perception of global moral responsibility and failing to seriously engage with international conflicts.

When brands avoid addressing significant atrocities, such as those in Gaza and Lebanon, they contribute to a culture of selective visibility, where market-driven priorities overshadow a genuine commitment to global justice. The increasing consumer activism, especially among young adults who engage in 'cancel culture' against brands or public figures silent on issues like Palestine, reflects a growing demand for political engagement. This trend highlights the need for brands to critically examine their role as cultural intermediaries and consider the ethical consequences of their decisions in shaping public discourse, particularly in terms of which issues they choose to amplify or ignore.

Finally, I advocate for a rethinking of the ethical responsibilities tied to visibility, emphasizing the significant role brands play as mediators of public discourse. Both visibility and invisibility have profound ethical implications, influencing whether social realities are empowered or marginalized. I call for a shift in brand engagement strategies, moving away from transactional approaches toward a more reflexive and dialogic model that emphasizes social impact. Brands must recognize their role as cultural producers, ensuring that their activism is not only rhetorically effective but also structurally transformative, aligning with the ethical expectations of a socially conscious audience.

Note

1 In 2022, Ben & Jerry's took legal action against Unilever to prevent the sale of its distribution rights in Israel. Unilever ultimately sold these rights to its existing local partner, who now sells the ice cream under a slightly modified brand. This conflict has contributed to Unilever's recent announcement to divest the Ben & Jerry's division by 2025 (Karaian, 2024).

References

Accenture. (2021). *Put your money where your mouth purpose is*. https://web.archive.org/web/20230130153122/https://www.accenture.com/_acnmedia/PDF-152/Accenture-POV-04-Put-Your-Money-Where-Your-PurposeIs.pdf

Adorno, T.W. (1973). *Negative dialectics*. Germany: Routledge & Kegan Paul.

Adorno, T.W. (2014). *Lectures on negative dialectics: Fragments of a lecture course* 1965/1966. Germany: Polity Press.

Ahmad, F., Guzmán, F. & Al-Emran, M (2024). Brand activism and the consequence of woke washing. *Journal of Business Research*, 170, 114362.

Airbnb. (2017). *Acceptance starts with all of us*. https://twitter.com/Airbnb/status/828394637874171904

Airbnb. (2022). *Host people fleeing Ukraine*. Airbnb.org. https://www.airbnb.org/help-ukraine (Accessed: January 15, 2024).

Alexander, P. (2015). *Corporate social irresponsibility*. London: Routledge.

Arvidsson, A. (2006). *Brands: Meaning and value in media culture*. London: Routledge.

Banerjee, S.B. (2008). Corporate social responsibility: The good, the bad and the ugly. *Critical Sociology*, 34(1), 51–79.

Banet-Weiser, S. (2012). *Authentic™: The politics of ambivalence in a brand culture*. New York: NYU Press.

Barthes, R. (1964). *Elements of semiology*. New York: Hill and Wang.

Baudrillard, J. (1994). Simulacra and simulation. University of Michigan Press. (Originally published in 1981.)

Bauman, Z. (2007). *Consuming life*. Cambridge: Polity Press.

Ben & Jerry's. (2023, May 18). *Ben & Jerry's will end sales of our ice cream in the Occupied Palestinian Territory*. Ben & Jerry's. https://www.benjerry.com/about-us/media-center/opt-statement

Bennett, W.L., & Segerberg, A. (2012). The logic of connective action: Digital media and the personalization of contentious politics. *Information, Communication & Society*, 15(5), 739–768.

Bhagwat, Y., Warren, N.L., Beck, J.T., & Watson IV, G.F. (2020). Corporate sociopolitical activism and firm value. *Journal of Marketing*, 84(5), 1–21.

Bloom, P. (2017). Empathy and its discontents. *Trends in Cognitive Sciences*, 21(1), 24–31.

Boltanski, L. (1999). *Distant suffering: Morality, media, and politics*. Cambridge: Cambridge University Press.

Boltanski, L. (2005). *The new spirit of capitalism*. Brooklyn: Verso.

Bourne, C. (2020). *Trust, Power and Public Relations in Financial Markets*. London: Routledge.

Boyd, D., McGarry, B.M., & Clarke, T.B. (2016). Exploring the empowering and paradoxical relationship between social media and CSR activism. *Journal of Business Research*, 69(9), 2739–2746.

Braun, V., & Clarke, V. (2022). *Thematic analysis: A practical guide*. London: SAGE Publications.

Buscaglia, S. (2023, December 29). *Milano, blitz di Ultima Generazione in Galleria: gli attivisti imbrattano l'albero di Gucci. E l'azienda non toglie la vernice: «Spunto di riflessione collettiva». Corriere Della Sera*. https://milano.corriere.it/notizie/cronaca/23_dicembre_29/milano-blitz-di-ultima-generazione-in-galleria-gli-attivisti-imbrattano-con-la-vernice-arancione-l-albero-di-gucci-776f7278-bd4b-4258-8b2d-20e21d00fxlk.shtml

Business & Human Rights Resource Centre. (2023). *Ukraine: McDonald's & KFC give away food and open kitchens for the military need despite Russian military invasion - Business & Human Rights Resource Centre*. https://www.business-humanrights.org/en/latest-news/ukraine-mcdonalds-kfc-give-away-food-and-open-kitchens-for-the-military-need-despite-russian-military-invasion/ (Accessed: January 15, 2024).

Cammarota, A., D'Arco, M., Marino, V., & Resciniti, R. (2023). BRAND ACTIVISM: A literature review and future research agenda. *International Journal of Consumer Studies*, 47(5), 1669–1691. https://doi.org/10.1111/ijcs.12967

Carroll, A. B., & Brown, J. A. (2018). Corporate social responsibility: A review of current concepts, research, and issues. *Corporate Social Responsibility*, 39–69.

Chouliaraki, L. (2006). *The spectatorship of suffering*. London: SAGE Publications.

Chouliaraki, L. (2012). The theatricality of humanitarianism: A critique of celebrity advocacy. *Communication and Critical/Cultural Studies, 9*(1), 1–21. https://doi.org/10.1080/14791420.2011.637055

Chouliaraki, L. (2013). *The ironic spectator: Solidarity in the age of post-humanitarianism*. Cambridge: Polity Press.

Christen, M., van Schaik, C., Fischer, J., Huppenbauer, M., & Tanner, C. (Eds.). (2016). *Empirically informed ethics: Morality between facts and norms*. Cham: Springer International Publishing.

Chughtai, A., Ali, M., & Nolan, D. (2023, December 15). Boycotts and protests – how are people around the world defying Israel? *Al Jazeera*. https://www.aljazeera.com/news/2023/12/15/boycotts-and-protests-how-are-people-around-the-world-defying-israel

Crane, A., & Glozer, S. (2016). Researching corporate social responsibility communication: Themes, opportunities and challenges. *Journal of Management Studies*, 53(7), 1223–1252.

Cronin, A.M. (2018). *Public relations capitalism: Promotional culture, publics and commercial democracy*. Cham: Springer.

Deuze, M. (2011). Media life. *Media, Culture & Society*, 33(1), 137–148.

Drumwright, M.E., & Murphy, P.E. (2004). How advertising practitioners view ethics: Moral muteness, moral myopia, and moral imagination. *Journal of Advertising*, 33(2), 7–24.

Durbin, D.-A. (2023, October 18). Starbucks, workers United union sue each other in standoff over pro-Palestinian social media post. *AP News*. https://apnews.com/article/starbucks-workers-united-union-lawsuit-israel-palestinian-f212a994fef67f122854a4df7e5d13f5

Eco, U. (1976). *A theory of semiotics*. Bloomington: Indiana University Press.

Eco, U. (1994). *The role of the reader: Explorations in the semiotics of texts*. Bloomington: Indiana University Press.

Edelman (2024). Trust Barometer: Special Report - brand and politics. https://www.edelman.com/trust/2024/trust-barometer/special-report-brand. Date Accessed 13 Nov. 2024.

Edwards, L. (2010). Authenticity in organizational context: Fragmentation, contradiction and loss of control. *Journal of Communication Management, 14*(3), 192–205. https://doi.org/10.1108/13632541011064481

Edwards, L., Bourne, C., Cabañes, J. V. A., & Castro, G. (Eds.). (2025). *The Sage Handbook of promotional culture and society*. London: SAGE Publications Ltd.

Fiske, J. (1987). *Television culture*. London: Methuen.

Floch, J.M., Sherry, J.F., & Bodkin, R.O. (2001). *Semiotics, marketing and communication: Beneath the signs, the strategies*. New York: Palgrave.
Foucault, M. (1977). *Discipline and punish: The birth of the prison*. New York: Vintage Books.
Fraser, N. (2023). *Cannibal capitalism: How our system is devouring democracy, care, and the planet - and what we can do about it*. Brooklyn: Verso Books.
Habermas, J. (1989). *The structural transformation of the public sphere. An inquiry into a category of Bourgeois society*. Cambridge, MA: MIT Press.
Hale, E. (2023, October 13). After outcry over Ukraine, big business muted on Israel-Hamas war. *Al Jazeera*. https://www.aljazeera.com/economy/2023/10/13/after-outcry-over-ukraine-big-business-muted-on-israel-hamas-war
Hall, S. (1973). *Encoding and decoding in the television discourse*. Centre for Cultural Studies, University of Birmingham, Birmingham.
Hall, S. (1997). *Representation: Cultural representations and signifying* practices. London: SAGE.
Hardt, M., & Negri, A. (2000). *Empire*. Harvard University Press. https://doi.org/10.2307/j.ctvjnrw54.
Hardy, J. (2021). *Branded content: The fateful merging of media and marketing*. London: Routledge.
Han, B. (2018). *The expulsion of the other: Society, perception and communication today*. Germany: Polity Press.
Han, B.-C. (2015). *The burnout society*. Stanford, CA: Stanford University Press.
Hollebeek, L., Glynn, M., & Brodie, R. (2014). Consumer brand engagement in social media: Conceptualization, scale development and validation. *Journal of Interactive Marketing*, 28, 149–165.
Holt, D.B. (2012a). Constructing sustainable consumption: From ethical values to the cultural transformation of unsustainable markets. *The ANNALS of the American Academy of Political and Social Science*, 644(1), 236–255.
Holt, D.B. (2012b). Cultural brand strategy. In *Handbook of marketing strategy*, p. 306. Northampton, MA: Edward Elgar Publishing.
Hopkins, P. (2017). *Mass moralizing: Marketing and moral storytelling*. Lanham, MD: Lexington Books.
Illouz, E. (2007). *Cold intimacies: The making of emotional capitalism*. Cambridge: Polity Press.
Javed, S. (2022, March 11). *From McDonald's to Prada, these are the brands that have stopped selling in Russia*. Independent. https://www.independent.co.uk/life-style/brands-russia-boycott-sanctions-companies-b2033887.html
Johnstone, M.L., & Tan, L.P. (2015). Exploring the gap between consumers' green rhetoric and purchasing behaviour. *Journal of Business Ethics*, 132, 311–328.
Jordan, D. (2023, December 12). Zara says it regrets Gaza images misunderstanding. *BBC*. https://www.bbc.co.uk/news/business-67690447
Karaian, J. (2024, Autumn 3). Unilever to *c*ut 7,500 *j*obs and *s*pin *o*ff Ben & Jerry's Ice Cream Unit. *New York Times*. https://www.nytimes.com/2024/03/19/business/unilever-ben-jerrys-job-cuts.html
Kazmi, B. A., Leca, B., & Naccache, P. (2016). Is corporate social responsibility a new spirit of capitalism?. *Organization, 23*(5), 742–762.
Keller, K.L., (2003). Brand synthesis: The multidimensionality of brand knowledge. *Journal of Consumer Research*, 29(4), 595–600.

Khamis, S. (2020). *Branding diversity: New advertising and cultural strategies*. London: Routledge.

Klein, N. (2000). *No LOGO*. London: Picador.

Korschun, D. (2021). Brand activism is here to stay: Here's why. *NIM Marketing Intelligence Review, 13*(2), 10–17.

Kotler, P., & Lee, N. (2005). *Corporate social responsibility: Doing the most good for your company and your cause*. Hoboken, NJ: John Wiley & Sons.

Kotler, P., & Sarkar, C. (2017). Finally, brand activism. *The Marketing Journal*, 9. https://www.marketingjournal.org/finally-brand-activism-philip-kotler-and-christian-sarkar/.

Kotler, P., & Sarkar, C. (2018). Stand for something: Brand activism at Nike. *The Marketing Journal*, 8(9). https://www.marketingjournal.org/stand-for-something-brand-activism-at-nike-christian-sarkar-and-philip-kotler/

Kozinets, R.V., & Jenkins, H. (2022). Consumer movements, brand activism, and the participatory politics of media: A conversation. *Journal of Consumer Culture*, 22(1), 264–282. https://doi.org/10.1177/14695405211013993

Lazarsfeld, P.F., & Merton, R.K. (1948). Mass communication, popular taste, and organized social action. In L. Bryson (Ed.), *The Communication of Ideas* (pp. 95–118). New York: Harper & Row.

Lekakis, E.J. (2022). *Consumer activism: Promotional culture and resistance*. London: SAGE Publications.

Manfredi-Sánchez, J.L. (2019). Brand activism. *Communication and Society*, 32(4), 343–359.

Marrone, G. (2007). *Il discorso di marca. Modelli semiotici per il branding* (Vol. 1, pp. 1–370). Rome, Italy: Laterza.

McDonalds. (2022). *McDonald's announces update on operations in Ukraine*. https://corporate.mcdonalds.com/corpmcd/our-stories/article/ukraine-reopen.html (Accessed: January 15, 2024).

Mckinsey. (2021) *Great Expectations: Navigating challenging stakeholder expectations of brands*. https://web.archive.org/web/20230130154229/https://www.mckinsey.com/industries/consumer-packaged-goods/our-insights/great-expectations-navigating-challenging-stakeholder-expectations-of-brands

McQuail, D. (2010). *McQuail's mass communication theory* (6th ed.). London: SAGE Publications.

MilanoToday. (2023). *È polemica sull'albero di Natale di Gucci in Galleria*. MilanoToday (2023, December 4). https://www.milanotoday.it/attualita/albero--natale-gucci-polemiche-2023-.html

Morley, D. (2003). *Television, audiences and cultural studies*. Milton Park, UK: Taylor & Francis.

Mukherjee, R., & Banet-Weiser, S. (Eds.). (2012). *Commodity activism: Cultural resistance in neoliberal times*. New York: NYU Press.

Nike (2020). *For Once, Don't Do It*. https://youtu.be/drcO2V2m7lw?si=Nek3shdhNnT70B-I. Accessed 13 Nov 2024.

Oswald, L.R. (2012). *Marketing semiotics: Signs, strategies, and brand value*. Oxford: Oxford University Press.

Oswald, L.R. (2015). The structural semiotics paradigm for marketing research: Theory, methodology, and case analysis. *Semiotica*, 2015(205), 115–148. https://doi.org/10.1515/sem-2015-0005

Powell, S. (2011). The nexus between ethical corporate marketing, ethical corporate identity and corporate social responsibility: An internal organisational perspective. *European Journal of Marketing*, 45(9/10), 1365–1379.

Rawls, J. (1971). *A theory of justice*. Cambridge, MA: Harvard University Press.

Sachdeva, M. (2023, December 12). Zara faces boycott calls over campaign 'mocking' Gaza victims. *Independent*. https://www.independent.co.uk/life-style/fashion/zara-the-jacket-campaign-gaza-boycott-b2462420.html

Salamone, L. (2024, January 2). Gucci Christmas tree: Vandalism. *Nss Magazine*. https://www.nssmag.com/en/fashion/35320/aveva-senso-imbrattare-l-albero-di-gucci-a-milano

Scherer, A.G., Palazzo, G., & Seidl, D. (2013). Managing legitimacy in complex and heterogeneous environments: Sustainable development in a globalized world. *Journal of Management Studies*, 50(2), 259–284.

Sennett, R. (1998). *The corrosion of character: The personal consequences of work in the new capitalism*. New York: W.W. Norton & Company.

Serazio, M. (2015). Selling (digital) millennials: The social construction and technological bias of a consumer generation. *Television & New Media*, 16(7), 599–615.

Sibai, O., Mimoun, L., & Boukis, A. (2021). Authenticating brand activism: Negotiating the boundaries of free speech to make a change. *Psychology & Marketing*, 38(10), 1651–1669.

Silverstone, R. (2002). Complicity and collusion in the mediation of everyday life. *New Literary History*, 33(4), 761–780.

Singer, P. (1972). Famine, affluence, and morality. *Philosophy & Public Affairs*, 1(3), 229–243.

Sobande, F. (2019). Woke-washing: "Intersectional" femvertising and branding "woke" bravery. *European Journal of Marketing*, 54(11), 2723–2745.

Sobande, F. (2023). *CONSUMING CRISIS: Commodifying care and covid-19*. London: SAGE.

Sobande, F. (2024). *Big brands are watching you: Marketing social justice and digital culture*. Oakland, CA: University of California Press.

Sontag, S. (2003). *Regarding the pain of others*. London: Picador.

Speed, M. (2024, January 16). Ben & Jerry's calls for permanent ceasefire in Gaza. *Financial Times*. https://on.ft.com/4csWh6e

Starbucks. (2018). *Starbucks Stories: 'They are lifesaving': Starbucks offers expanded benefits for trans people*. https://stories.starbucks.com/stories/2018/they-are-life-saving-starbucks-offers-expanded-benefits-for-trans-people/ (Accessed January 15, 2024).

Taylor, C. (2018). *The ethics of authenticity*. Cambridge, MA: Harvard University Press.

Tessman, L. (2014). *Moral failure: On the impossible demands of morality*. Oxford: Oxford University Press.

Uldam, J. (2018). Social media visibility: Challenges to activism. *Media, Culture & Society*, 40(1), 41–58.

Vredenburg, J., Kapitan, S., Spry, A., & Kemper, J.A. (2020). Brands taking a stand: Authentic brand activism or woke washing? *Journal of Public Policy & Marketing*, 39(4), 444–460.

Weissbrot, A. (2023, October 10). How brands are responding to the Israel-Gaza war. *PR Week Global*. https://www.prweek.com/article/1840277/brands-responding-israel-gaza-war

West, E., & McAllister, M.P. (Eds.). (2023). *The Routledge companion to advertising and promotional culture*. London: Routledge.

Zyglidopoulos, S.C., Georgiadis, A.P., Carroll, C.E., & Siegel, D.S. (2019). Does media attention drive corporate social responsibility? *Journal of Business Ethics*, 160(3), 725–740.

2 The Taxonomy of the Activist Brand

Visionary, Sensitive, and Reflexive Brands

Empathy, commonly understood as the ability to comprehend and share the feelings of others (Read, 2019), is a fundamental element of human nature. It enables us to connect with others, build relationships and foster a sense of community (Betzler, 2019; Slote, 2007). In the realm of marketing, empathy has been employed as a strategic tool to deepen audience engagement and establish a more emotional and personal bond with consumers (Hutchins and Rodriguez, 2018; Noddings, 2012). In brand activism, empathy serves as a communicative strategy to inspire involvement and drive impactful change (Kozinets and Jenkins, 2021, p. 4). However, the application of empathy in marketing and advertising has stirred debate concerning the true motivations of brands (Key et al., 2021). Brands encourage consumers to "develop empathy and care for distant others in need and to participate in demonstrations, the concern with global injustice is simultaneously turned into an individualized opportunity for entrepreneurial personal growth" (Orgad and Gill, 2022, p. 133). This raises two pertinent questions.

The first looks at the strategic use of empathy in activist brand campaigns and its contribution to moral complacency among consumers. This complacency manifests when consumers believe that their engagement with a brand, such as through purchases or social media interactions, constitutes a sufficient contribution to social causes. The second question investigates how empathetic narratives crafted by brands in their activism campaigns, while successful in raising awareness and forging emotional connections, might fail to motivate consumers to engage in meaningful, direct actions that go beyond consumption. Therefore, to analyze these campaigns is crucial to deconstruct the language used in activist brand campaigns that adopt empathetic narratives, with particular attention to how these narratives contribute to structuring public morality. Such analysis helps to discern whether these campaigns earnestly align with ethical principles or merely employ them as a strategic tool to enhance brand image within the existing capitalist framework.

In developing my answer to these two questions, I adopt a three-stage approach.

DOI: 10.4324/9781003105893-2

The first stage of the analysis involves a critical examination of the theoretical debate around the role of advertising in developing empathy, advocating to move away from abstract discussions about a brand's moral standing to analyze empathic representations of the other through case studies. This orientation acknowledges cultural influences that shape individual experiences and their interpretations, enabling a more comprehensive understanding of how empathy is employed and perceived in the context of brand narratives.

In the second stage, I conduct an analysis of specific activist brand campaigns from 2017 to 2022, using case studies to focus these narratives are strategically constructed to evoke moral competence in relation to the other. This analysis illustrates how the moral dilemmas presented in these campaigns demand varying levels of moral agency from viewers, compelling them to take on greater responsibility for their ethical judgments and actions. Through this process, I develop a taxonomy of activist brands, categorizing the interpretative frameworks that consumers may engage with when exposed to these campaigns, and examining how these frameworks influence their moral perceptions and behaviors.

Finally, in the third stage, I contend that advertisers should exercise caution when using empathic narratives to establish a moral high ground. Instead, brands should strive to create connections with their audience. This demands a more profound understanding of the vulnerabilities and limitations of empathy, especially in contexts where viewers are faced with complex moral judgments. This final stage of the argument thus highlights the ethical responsibilities of brands in their pursuit of activism and the need for a conscientious approach to the use of empathy in advertising.

Questioning the Link between Empathy and Moral Action

Empathy, defined as a cognitive and affective state achieved through mental exercises such as "putting oneself in another's shoes," allows an individual to experience the thoughts and feelings of another person (Oxley, 2011, p. 3). The concept originated from the German word Einfühlung, translating to "projecting oneself into another context" (Jacob, 2011, p. 520). Initially used in aesthetics, empathy involved the viewer projecting their feelings onto a work of art to appreciate it fully (Lanzoni, 2018, p. 76). The understanding of empathy expanded through the works of philosophers like David Hume and Adam Smith, who explored the individual's ability to understand and share another's pain and perspective (Sugden, 2002). Hume's (1978) phrase, "The minds of men are mirrors to each other," (p. 365) illustrates the idea that individuals' thoughts and feelings can resonate and reflect in their interactions, being recreated at different levels of mediation.

Recent criticisms, however, have challenged this conventional perspective (Bloom, 2016). The varying interpretations of empathy often hinge on the recognition of the other person (Hoffmann, 2000; Shoemaker, 2017), sparking discussions about whether empathy entails seeing the other as 'someone who is like me' or 'someone who is like people in general.' This debate becomes particularly convoluted in the context of media representations of a distant other (Boltanski, 1999; Silverstone, 2002), and when media are used to elicit specific emotional responses (Chouliaraki, 2008). While empathy fundamentally involves an individual's capacity to resonate with others through various means, including language, visuals, and sensory input, the encounter with mediated empathy can present challenges. Such mediated empathy often lacks mutual understanding, making it difficult for individuals to fully adopt the perspective of the other. This situation can lead to a distorted or incomplete understanding of others' experiences, highlighting the need for an inquiry into empathy in media representations.

Empathy can be viewed as a means of bridging the gap between oneself and another (Sartre, 1943), functioning as a social process and a form of social cognition. It enables engagement with others, understanding of their perspectives, and sharing of their feelings (Gangopadhyay, 2014). However, the question creeps in whether true empathy is possible without the projection of one's own feelings and emotions onto the other. From a phenomenological standpoint, empathy provides immediate access to another's emotions, aiding in understanding their experiences and perceptions, even when they differ from our own (Zahavi, 2014, p. 152). Thus, empathy is more than just projecting one's emotions; it is an intentional act of recognizing and responding to others' emotions within a shared context. This understanding positions empathy as a form of knowledge, a conscious effort to connect with and comprehend the emotional states of others in a meaningful way.

Activist brand campaigns that employ empathic narratives to represent the other can evoke strong emotional responses, but their potential unintended consequences must be scrutinized. Ahmed (2013, p. 36), in "The Cultural Politics of Emotion," explores how the construction of the other is influenced by power dynamics and social norms, whereby emotions shape our perceptions and interactions and are often used to maintain power structures. An excessive focus on individual experiences and emotions runs the risk of depoliticization (Matthiesen and Klitmøller, 2019, p. 188), potentially overlooking systemic factors underpinning social issues.

Reflecting on the paradox of complacency and inaction, empathy emerges not merely as an emotional response but as a social construct intertwined with moral judgments and perceptions (Calhoun, 1991, pp. 231–233). Morality is an integral part of the human experience, shaping self-conception and world interactions. In contemporary contexts with blurred ethical boundaries, the role of empathy in moral decision-making gains prominence (Honneth, 2014). However, the limitations of empathy become apparent, especially in its capacity to connect meaningfully with the other. Empathy can be subject to superficial understandings if not coupled with critical analysis of social and cultural dynamics.

The necessity for a dialectical approach to empathy in brand activism is thus clear. It is crucial to move beyond mere emotional resonance to actions that address broader structural realities. Moral action involves understanding systemic causes and taking substantive steps beyond brand-driven campaigns. This requires a critical analysis of empathic narratives in brand activism, assessing their alignment with genuine moral action and their contribution to, or hindrance of, social justice and ethical responsibility.

Moralizing the Other

To collect the data for this analysis, a purposive sampling method was utilized, concentrating on press coverage in UK and US newspapers. The search strategy incorporated specific keywords, including 'brand activism,' 'campaign,' and 'advertising,' to identify relevant articles and features. The timeframe for this study was deliberately chosen, starting from 2017—coinciding with former US President Trump's inauguration speech, a period marked by its political prominence—to 2022, when the writing of this analysis commenced. The choice of 2017 as the starting point was strategic, particularly due to the Super Bowl event in February of that year which witnessed a notable surge in politicized commercials. This event marked a transformative moment in the discourse of brand activism, providing a compelling entry point for this study. The five-year period of comprehensive data collection concluded in 2022; the result is a robust overview of the developments and tendencies in brand activism during this significant era.

Following an initial review of the news articles, a dataset comprising the most influential and widely discussed activist brand campaigns was created. This selection was further refined by examining the social media channels of the involved brands, focusing on those campaigns that not only garnered substantial media attention but also stimulated considerable engagement online. This dual approach of analyzing both traditional media and digital platforms provided a more layered understanding of the public reception and impact of these campaigns. It offered insights into how these brand initiatives resonated with audiences and the extent to which they influenced discussions and interactions in both digital and wider social contexts.

To analyze the data systematically, I employed a reflexive thematic analysis approach as detailed by Clarke and Brown (2022), complemented by a critical phenomenological framework (Magrì and McQueen, 2023). This combined methodology was instrumental in uncovering and interpreting the moral universe (Cohen, 2010, p. 21) embedded within activist brand campaigns. The moral universe of an activist brand campaign refers to the ethical and moral values and beliefs that inform our judgments about what is just or unjust, right or wrong. This moral universe shapes how brands construct their narratives and engage with societal issues, influencing societal norms, values, and the public's perception of the other (Borgerson and Schroeder,

2002). In the context of brand activism, the moral universe encompasses the ethical principles and positions a brand adopts and communicates through its campaigns.

The following three levels represent various brand narrative types employed in activist brand campaigns to evoke empathy toward the other. Each identified level demonstrates a distinct approach to create moral competence, depending on the narrative strategy used to forge an empathic connection with the audience. Moral competence, as defined by Rest (1979), refers to the viewer's ability to recognize, understand, and act upon moral principles and ethical considerations in relation to the other. It involves the capacity to discern right from wrong and make decisions that reflect ethical responsibility. I argue that these narratives provide an ontological space where viewers can practice and develop their moral skills at varying levels of cognitive competency (Kohlberg, 1981).

This ontological space, created by the brand narratives, serves as a virtual environment where individuals can engage with moral dilemmas, reflect on ethical issues, and cultivate their ability to respond empathetically and responsibly to the needs and experiences of others. This process allows viewers to enhance their moral competence, deepening their understanding of and commitment to ethical values and actions in real-world contexts. The significance of these levels lies in their ability to show that the analyzed advertisements not only address moral issues in a profound and meaningful way but also employ varying levels of moral understanding of the other. These levels also reflect the brand's approach to addressing social issues and its impact on shaping public discourse and attitudes.

Visionary Brand Activism: Feeling the Other

In the context of brand activism, a strong moral perspective in addressing present societal issues is conveyed through an emotional vision, which refers to a brand's portrayal of a desired moral idea about the way the world should be or appear. This vision encapsulates the brand's ideals, values, and aspirations for societal change, aiming to resonate with the viewer's sense of morality and ethics. Empathy plays a central role in this, as it can facilitate a connection between the brand and the viewer in terms of moral understanding. By appealing to the viewer's emotions and moral sensibilities, the brand's vision seeks to inspire, motivate, and engage individuals in a shared pursuit of a better, more just society. When a brand is capable of improving the customer's moral competence, it assumes the role of an agent that can help in making difficult choices. The brand presents a moral vision that seeks to stimulate the viewer's thinking and to consider predefined moral actions. However, the narrative constructed by the brand is prescriptive and the viewer's agency at the narrative level is limited to simply accepting or rejecting the brand's vision.

By presenting a singular view of what is morally right or wrong, these campaigns risk oversimplifying problems and alienating those who may have different perspectives or experiences. Such campaigns often fail to acknowledge the diversity of views and experiences that exist in the world (Orgad and Gill, 2022, p. 26). They often lack nuance in the messaging, which may be counterproductive in promoting meaningful social change. While the prescriptive approach of visionary brands can help to inspire action and mobilize support, it is important to recognize that there are often multiple ways of addressing social and environmental issues. By heeding the diversity of views and experiences, these brands would be able to foster a sense of inclusivity and dialogue that can facilitate more effective and sustainable solutions.

The adequacy of a visionary brand's moral discourse of reality is not a straightforward issue; it is rather more necessary to examine the conditions of discourse production that make it appear so. One such condition concerns the logic of 'us vs them' that both Patagonia and Ben & Jerry's employ in their campaigns. As Weitzner (2022) notes, it is a mistake for managers of publicly traded companies to think of their shareholders as part of an 'us' group and everyone else as 'them.' However, this logic presents the brand as a savior and mythologizes current problems as a battle between good and evil, lending the narrative a semi-religious tone. As such, the brand's moral vision tends to promote a particular way of thinking, feeling or acting without providing moral choices, limiting the subjectivity of the viewer. The moral vision presented by the brand is thus the only voice, exemplifying its prescriptive nature.

The narrative of visionary brands exhibits four recurring characteristics:

- Ethical Possibility: The brand's narrative conveys a moral imperative, suggesting that people must engage in certain actions or behaviors. For instance, Patagonia and Ben & Jerry's are proactive in urging individuals to engage in specific actions to address social and environmental issues, presenting a somewhat one-dimensional view of morality.
- Singular Space-Time Narrative: In this narrative structure, the brand positions itself as the sole protagonist, distancing the viewer from directly connecting with the social cause it is addressing. By offering a singular perspective on ethical behavior, visionary brands risk simplifying social ocmplexity and may not fully accommodate the diverse ways in which individuals interpret and engage with ethical challenges.
- Non-Dialectical Brand Identification: While the narrative encourages the viewer to identify with the brand, it presents a non-dialectical vision. This approach implies a self-identification with the brand's perspective, often at the expense of the viewer's subjective representation or interpretative agency. This narrative provides clear, actionable directives, which can be highly effective in motivating consumer participation in these causes.
- Undefined or Abstract 'Other': Vulnerable groups or those suffering from injustice are often depicted in a vague or abstract manner. For example,

a brand might focus on environmental preservation and restoration without specifically addressing the plight of indigenous communities or populations directly impacted by climate change.

A striking characteristic of these visionary brands is that their narratives convey a sense of ethical certainty in their campaigns. This means that they often present their actions as inherently ethical, regardless of whether viewers agree with their values or goals. In other words, these brands assume a certain level of ethical authority that is independent of audience evaluations or opinions. This is a notable departure from traditional marketing which typically seeks to cater to audience preferences and tastes. Instead, visionary brands often seek to shape audience perspectives and priorities, positioning themselves as moral and ethical guides for viewers. This approach can be seen as an attempt to create a sense of trust and authority, but it can also be viewed as limiting because it may prevent viewers from fully engaging with the diversity of ethical issues ("pseudo-diversity" in Orgad and Gill, 2022, p. 43). As such, it is important to critically examine the ethical dispositions and assumptions underlying the narratives of visionary brands, and to consider the role that marketing plays in shaping our understanding of morality and ethical decision-making.

Sensitive Brand: Feeling for Others

In the context of brand activism, the ability of a brand to respond appropriately to various events and issues with a high degree of moral sensitivity is an indispensable component of its moral action. Such events and issues can often present ethical dilemmas with opposing considerations, making it difficult to make overtly evident moral judgments. As Jordan (2007, p. 326) notes, in these situations moral sensitivity is essential to arrive at ethical decisions. A brand's willingness to tackle urgent moral issues is a sign of its moral sensitivity which can be measured by its commitment to supporting those who have less power or responsibility, or even those who are in need. From this perspective, the cognitive-interpretive process, by which empathy is constructed with the viewer, is a key factor in the narratives of morally sensitive brands.

In contrast to brands with a moral vision, morally sensitive brands aim to cultivate morally correct thoughts, motives, and actions in their viewers without prescribing specific actions or behaviors. However, it is also possible for brands to demonstrate a lack of moral sensitivity by failing to consider the diverse cultural factors that may impact their customers. For example, social media backlash erupted (Thomas, 2018) when videos circulated of angry conservative consumers purportedly torching Nike sneakers (Abad-Santos, 2018) in response to the selection of Colin Kaepernick as a testimonial for the brand's 'Just Do It' campaign. In this context, one must question whether Nike demonstrated a lack of moral sensitivity and vision in their failure to consider the cultural implications of their decision.

I argue that the answer to this question is no. Nike's advertising campaigns focus on the moral implications of discrimination and promote the idea that sport can be a powerful tool for promoting equality and bringing people together (Papson and Goldman, 1998). This sets Nike apart from competitors who may not prioritize these issues in their advertising. In contrast to brands like Ben & Jerry's and Patagonia, Nike's campaigns aim to raise awareness about the harmful effects of prejudice and to advocate for solutions to social inequality rather than simply accepting or tolerating it. By presenting a positive and inclusive vision of the world, Nike contributes to a better understanding of how society should approach fairness and social justice.

In the narrative of morally sensitive brands, three recurrent features can be identified:

- Transition to Diverse Space-Time Narratives: There is a shift from a singular, uniform narrative to narratives that are more concrete, specific, diverse, and dynamic in their space-time dimensions. This approach allows for more varied storytelling that can resonate more deeply with different audiences.
- Evolution of Emotive Narratives: These brands are developing increasingly sophisticated visual and verbal narratives. These narratives are not just more elaborated but are also imbued with greater emotional power, enhancing their ability to connect with and move the audience on a deeper level.
- Personalization of the Other: In these narratives, the other is represented as the viewer themselves, along with their individual struggles and experiences. An outside narrator, speaking from beyond the story's world, helps create a conversation between the brand and the audience, making the connection feel more personal. This approach shifts the focus to the viewer's perspective, creating a sense of empathy and engagement.

In the construction of a morally sensitive brand narrative, there is an intriguing dynamic where the viewer is accorded a form of conditional personhood. This term refers to the social and political agency granted to the viewer as a participant in the narrative, albeit in a limited and somewhat prescribed manner. In such narratives, the viewer's role is acknowledged, but their capacity to act is often constrained within the narrative's framework. As a result, an external voice, such as that of Kaepernick, becomes essential for providing direction and meaning within the narrative. He is often portrayed in a way that blends the mythical with the relatable, positioning him as both a cultural outsider and someone familiar. This portrayal allows viewers to see themselves in the narrative, infusing a human quality into the brand that is often lacking in more abstract or morally visionary brand narratives.

These sensitive brand narratives employ an indirect moralizing strategy. They do not dictate a fixed set of moral values; instead, they foster empathy in a dialectical manner, engaging the viewer in a dynamic process of moral contemplation and realization. Such narratives are problematic, as they demonstrate the breadth and limitations of moral action available to the viewers. They invite the audience to engage with moral issues more reflectively and personally, rather than prescribing a one-size-fits-all moral stance. This approach to brand storytelling indicates a sophisticated understanding of moral action that recognizes the problems and varied interpretations of ethical behavior among viewers. In essence, morally sensitive brand narratives take a more layered approach to engaging audiences in ethical discourse and offer a space for viewers to explore and define their moral actions within the narrative context.

Reflexive Brand: Feeling with Others

Moral reflexivity refers to the conscious effort to consider oneself and others in all circumstances. When a brand adopts narratives based on moral principles and values that reflect changes in society, it demonstrates moral reflexivity. This commitment to doing good in the community and willingness to address contentious issues is in the public interest. It is important to note that reflexive branding is not limited to the promotion of social causes such as body positivity or toxic masculinity, as exemplified by Dove's campaigns on real beauty (see also Banet-Weiser, 2012, p. 40; Orgad and Gill, 2022, p. 25) and Gillette's advertisements (2019) addressing toxic masculinity (see also Khamis, 2020, pp. 45–48). Brands that demonstrate reflexivity may address a wide range of societal issues and do so in a way that reflects changes in public opinion.

This approach allows brands to adapt and respond to evolving societal values and concerns, making their messaging and actions more relevant and impactful. By engaging with various social issues, brands can position themselves as agents of social change, aligning their values and practices with the expectations and beliefs of their consumer base. This strategy not only helps in addressing societal issues but also cultivates a positive image among consumers who increasingly value social responsibility and moral integrity. Through reflexive branding, companies can demonstrate their commitment to contributing positively to society, developoing a stronger connection with consumers who seek brands that align with their ethical and moral principles.

In the narrative of the reflexive brand, three key elements stand out:

- Complexity and Multivocality in Narratives: There is a noticeable shift from traditional, linear advertising narratives to more sophisticated ones, incorporating multiple voices and emotive storytelling. A prime example is Dove's 'Real Beauty' campaigns in which everyday people are the focal point. This strategy invites the viewer to engage empathetically with societal issues, such as challenging unrealistic beauty standards, by presenting relatable, real-life scenarios.

- Empathy in Ordinary Life Experiences: Reflexive brands embed empathy in everyday life experiences, making their messages more relatable and universally applicable. This approach allows viewers to connect with broader, shared social movements, like the #MeToo movement or the conversation around toxic masculinity, as seen in Gillette's campaigns (Khamis, 2020, p. 46). By grounding their narratives in common experiences, these brands foster a sense of solidarity and collective action.
- Universal Moral Stance Through Engagement: The narrative of a reflexive brand often establishes a universal moral position in addressing self-care and confidence (Orgad and Gill 2022, p. 84). This is achieved through the brand's sustained and in-depth engagement with everyday moral issues, where the viewer is not just an observer but an active participant with unconditional agency. This involvement encourages the audience not only to contemplate but also to act on the moral issues, facilitating a connection between the brand's values and the viewer's personal ethics.

The reflexive brand narrative enables a universal moral posture in response to the moral problems that the brand addresses. The brand's ongoing, deep engagement with ordinary moral issues is facilitated by the viewer's involvement as an agent with unconditional moral agency. Unconditional moral agency requires viewers to employ their own moral imagination, providing them with a space for moral reflection that is not dependent on the brand's position. Viewers are expected to take responsibility based on personal experiences and to make judgments from a neutral and dispassionate perspective that is assumed to be free from the brand's cultural polarity. However, unconditional moral agency can become problematic when brands tackle controversial moral problems (e.g., abortion, racism) with the intention of gaining more visibility.

The Empathic Other

The representation of the Other's agency in the Visionary and Sensitive Brands plays a crucial role in this process of depoliticization of the other. It is not just about raising awareness, but also about how the other is portrayed and understood. The challenge lies in ensuring that this representation does not reduce the other to a mere subject of empathy but instead portrays them as individuals with agency and dignity. This more refined portrayal can cultivate a richer understanding and connection, encouraging not just empathy but also a compelling urge to take action. The representation of the other needs to move beyond stereotypical or superficial depictions which produce a simplistic understanding of social issues and inhibit meaningful action.

Furthermore, the representation of the other in these two categories of brand narratives must avoid perpetuating a sense of 'Otherness' that distances them from the audience. Instead, it should aim to bridge the gap between the viewer and the other and prioritize a sense of shared humanity and mutual respect. This approach can encourage viewers to feel empathy in addition to comprehending the interconnectedness of social issues and their own role in addressing them. The portrayal should encourage viewers to see the other not as distant victims but as individuals with whom they share common ground and for whom they can take concrete actions to support.

These levels all address moral narratives but rely on differing levels of moral competency. While empathy for others is central across all three categories, the first two (Visionary and Sensitive Brands) do not establish a direct causal link between empathy and moral action in the narrative. In the first category, the other is abstract or undefined, while in the second, the other is the self. Consequently, empathy is redirected toward the self, portrayed as an image of the vulnerable other. In the third category (Reflexive Brand), viewers can distinguish themselves from the brand which is no longer seen as an image of the self but as an image of the other, representing someone distinct from the self.

While these three identified levels raise questions regarding whether empathy can be translated into moral action (Matthiesen and Klitmøller, 2019), the hierarchy among these categories indicates that activist brand campaigns are more difficult than a single typology can reveal. Nevertheless, this hierarchy demonstrates that there is a significant problem with how empathy is translated into moral action, and it underlines the importance of examining the dynamic interaction between the brand narrative and the viewer's moral agency. Each level forms part of a hierarchical ontology (Heil and Heil, 2003) and represents a different level of engagement with the other; the level of moral competency required of the viewer increases with each category of the taxonomy. Therefore, this type of advertising can be seen as an interpretative space that allows viewers to practice their moral skills and engage with moral problems at different levels of competency.

As viewers engage with more convoluted moral problems, they are called upon to exercise a higher interpretative level to take more responsibility for their moral judgments and actions. Therefore, in this taxonomy, the different category of brand narratives can be seen as operating on different levels of moral engagement with the viewer. At the bottom of the hierarchy is a type of moral narrative that keeps the viewer at a distance from moral engagement, giving them no way to interact with the Other. In contrast, at the top of the hierarchy, the reflexive brand puts viewers in a position of reflexivity wherein they see the brand as a moral agent and are able to empathize with the vulnerable other.

Moral Action and the Other

It is worth exploring whether activist campaigns can employ empathy as a tool without necessarily resulting in moral action. Indeed, there may be cause for concern about what happens when empathy is not followed by moral action: could the appeal to empathy lead to an inaccurate assessment of the relative severity of different sorts of needs in the world, giving more weight to proximate, visible, and familiar demands? What does occur when empathy is not followed by moral action? The link between the use of empathy and the lack of moral action is grounded in two key aspects. First, morality is integral to distinguish between right and wrong and to evaluate the actions of others. Second, empathy is essential to motivate moral or selfless action. These aspects form the foundation of the argument presented in this section, which analyzes the interaction between empathy and moral action, seeking to unravel the intertwinement of our emotional responses and ethical decisions.

The major problem in the interaction between empathy and moral action arises from the complexities of adopting empathic narratives in activist brand campaigns and specifically how these narratives structure moral action toward others (Matthiesen and Klitmøller, 2019, pp. 186–189). While empathy is necessary to connect with the emotions and needs of others, the language used to represent the other in brand activism could paradoxically produce moral complacency and inaction. This paradoxical condition may fail to address the root causes of systemic issues and could foment moral complacency, thereby limiting the potential for meaningful change (Oxley, 2011). The problem of mediation is notably tied to our ability to empathize with others (Silverstone, 2013). Mediated communication, such as media representations, can significantly shape how we relate to and understand others. However, when we are exposed to media that solely represents individuals similar to us, it can reinforce our existing biases and limit our capacity to empathize with those who are different (Silverstone, 2002, p. 770). Therefore, the way in which brands articulate narratives of suffering, solidarity and moral responsibility (Chouliariaki, 2012, p. 9) holds significant influence in shaping how audiences perceive and engage with the distant other.

Moral action, as explained by Bauman (2007, p. 39), recognizes and acknowledges the other as individuals with their own unique experiences, perspectives and needs, deserving of respect and value. This attitude extends beyond merely identifying the existence of the other; it involves acting in ways that promote their well-being and autonomy, treating them as entities with inherent rights and dignity. This is particularly vital in activist brand campaigns, where there is a need to engage with the other not as tools to further marketing objectives, but as human beings worthy of ethical consideration. An analytical framework to evaluate the representation of the other in these campaigns is critical—it ensures that the narratives used by brands acknowledge as well as represent the other's experiences and perspectives in alignment with true ethical behavior and moral responsibility.

Key considerations include the level of respect with which their experiences are portrayed, and whether their voices are genuinely amplified or simply reduced to a backdrop for the brand's own narrative. This scrutiny of the other is crucial to understand the full impact of the campaign's moral universe on its audience. It sheds light on the relationship between the narratives crafted by brands, the moral values they espouse, and the tangible effects these narratives have on the lives of those they represent. Such an examination offers valuable insights into the ethical dimensions of brand activism, revealing how these narratives influence public perception and the potential implications for the lived realities of the Other. It consequently becomes apparent that more responsible and realistic storytelling in corporate approaches to social issues is paramount.

This analytical framework serves as a key tool in assessing whether brand narratives respect and accurately portray the other's experiences and perspectives, ensuring they are treated with the dignity and consideration they inherently deserve. In Chapter 1, we encountered three ethical problems—(In)visibility, Selective Empathy and Moralizing Empathy—that unearth profound moral concerns regarding the representation of the Other in brand activism. These problems not only highlight significant ethical dilemmas but also serve as valuable conceptual categories for examining how the other is portrayed and the potential consequences of those portrayals. Before proceeding to Chapter 3, it is important to demonstrate how the problematization of these ethical challenges provides a robust framework for analyzing the portrayal of the other and its implications for moral complacency and inaction. This framework will be then adopted in both Chapters 3 and 4.

Similar to ethical issues in graphic memoirs and visual representation (Habegger-Conti, 2019), the (In)visibility paradigm reveals the difficulty of making the other visible in brand narratives (Bhargava and Bedi, 2021). While visibility can raise awareness, it often involves curating stories to fit marketable narratives, potentially stripping them of their autonomy (Martínez García, 2023). This process risks oversimplifying or commodifying the real struggles and needs of the other (Hunt, 2019), reducing their experiences to consumable content. Conversely, the issue of invisibility arises when the true depth of the other's experiences (Dreher 2009; Zahavi, 2014) is overshadowed or omitted, leading to a superficial understanding of the issues (Minocher, 2019; Stanley, 2020).

Selective Empathy in brand activism complicates the portrayal of the other, as brands often demonstrate empathy selectively, aligning their campaigns with those causes that resonate with their consumer base or enhance their public image (Key et al., 2021; Romani et al., 2015). This selective strategy results in a skewed representation, where attention and support are primarily given to certain groups or issues deemed more marketable or less contentious. Consequently, less popular or more controversial causes, and the other associated with them, are neglected and remain in the shadows. This selective empathy not only overlooks the needs of these marginalized groups but also inadvertently reinforces existing societal biases (Xie et al., 2019). This limits the potential for raising awareness about a broader range of issues and fails to provide necessary support to all the individuals and communities affected by them (Chen, 2023).

Moralizing Empathy poses a significant ethical challenge in brand activism, particularly in the representation of the other. Brands often depict the other in a way that serves their narrative of moral righteousness or positive change (Bhargava and Bedi, 2021). This usually results in representations that are overly optimistic or simplistic, with a heavy emphasis on positive, feel-good aspects while neglecting the more difficult realities faced by the other. Such depictions risk reducing the other to tools for evoking moral satisfaction or a sense of moral superiority in the audience, rather than addressing their actual needs or the systemic challenges they encounter. This typifies how limited brand narratives can be in conveying the true complexities of the other's experiences.

The ethical problems in brand activism illuminate a critical divide between the cultural dimension of empathy, which often emphasizes emotional narratives about our commitment to vulnerable individuals, and the political dimension of solidarity, which often focuses on human vulnerability as an issue of injustice (Sobande, 2023, 2024; Vredenburg et al., 2020). Balancing a brand's commercial interests with an accurate portrayal of the other is a tricky task, and it raises questions about the true potential of brand activism to contribute to effective social change and ethical engagement. The nature of brand activism, driven predominantly by marketing objectives, frequently obscures the ability of brand narratives to honor and represent the other accurately and wholly (Wannow et al., 2023). Rigorous scrutiny of these narratives serves to unveil whether they act in the interest of those they represent or whether the other is depicted (Szablewska et al., 2020) to achieve corporate goals. Maintaining this critical eye ensures that brand narratives move beyond commercial gain toward meaningful and respectful contributions to social and ethical discourse.

The ethical responsibility inherent in crafting empathic narratives places a significant burden on advertisers to exercise caution in their storytelling techniques. This includes carefully considering the construction of their narratives, the imagery they choose and the rhetoric they deploy. Brands have a duty to create narratives that are not only engaging but also ethically responsible and respectful (Poulton, 2005). Their aim should be to foster a form of empathy that inspires informed and ethical action, rather than merely promoting passive consumerism (Carrigan and Attalla, 2001). However, marketers' consistent realization of this objective is subject to debate, primarily because such an approach can conflict with the profit-driven motives that uphold and fuel capitalism (Husted and Allen, 2000). While this critique is not the central theme of this book, it does warrant further exploration. This exploration is undertaken in Chapter 4 through interviews with brand managers responsible for these activist brand campaigns, providing an insight into the challenges of balancing ethical storytelling with commercial objectives.

Recognizing that empathy, while a necessary component of moral action, is not sufficient on its own and should be complemented by moral principles and values is important. However, as I pointed out at the beginning of the chapter, there is a negative dialectical tension between genuine empathy, social responsibility and the profit-driven imperatives of capitalism. Efforts to reconcile these contradictory elements within the capitalist framework risk masking systemic issues and power imbalances. The tension between them underscores the challenges in aligning empathetic narratives with true social responsibility in brand activism, raising questions about the efficacy of these efforts in effecting real social change. A critical examination of the utilization of empathy in brand campaigns should ensure that brand activism goes beyond superficial engagement and contributes meaningfully to addressing the root causes of social issues within the broader ethical and systemic contexts.

The idea of combating social injustice by setting higher moral standards for advertising storytelling might seem promising, but it is somewhat illusory. In *Contingency, Irony, and Solidarity*, Rorty (1989) challenges the traditional view of moral progress being tied to the enforcement of specific normative principles. Instead, Rorty argues that true progress in society is more effectively achieved through the reduction or elimination of social injustices. This argument is particularly relevant when considering the role of advertising in addressing social issues. The journey toward a morally progressive society, therefore, involves a continuous effort to confront and reduce injustices, rather than to rely solely on the establishment of specific moral guidelines for advertisers. This is a more pragmatic approach to social change, one that prioritizes tangible actions and outcomes over conforming to idealized moral standards.

Understanding that empathy alone is insufficient for systemic change is crucial for achieving genuine moral progress. While empathy heightens awareness and deepens understanding of social issues, it must be accompanied by actionable strategies and systemic interventions to tackle the root causes of injustice effectively (Decety, 2021; Decety and Cowell, 2015). This perspective necessitates a paradigm shift in the role of advertising in social change, extending its function beyond eliciting empathetic responses to contributing meaningfully to the discourse on social injustice and systemic change (Kamal et al., 2022). Advertisers and brands, therefore, should leverage empathy not as an end goal but as a catalyst for more meaningful engagement and impactful action. By moving beyond superficial empathetic connections and actively participating in and advocating for systemic solutions, advertising can play a substantial role in driving meaningful and lasting moral progress in society (Bartsch and Kloß, 2018). However, it is necessary to remain skeptical of the extent to which corporations, inherently driven by profit, can fulfill such a role in society and align with the goals of social justice and systemic change.

In conclusion, this chapter laid out a three-stage argument on the role of activist brand campaigns in fostering empathy and moral action among audiences. The first stage provided an overview of the theoretical debate surrounding advertising's role in promoting empathy. The focus was on the limitations of empathy, especially within mediated contexts. Analyzing empathic narratives to understand the construction of the other reveals brand positioning and how it influences audience perception and emotional engagement with social issues.

The second stage of analysis examines specific activist brand campaigns from 2017 to 2022, drawing on case studies to assess how effectively these campaigns evoke moral competence. The study identifies three categories of brand narratives, each eliciting different levels of moral engagement from the viewer. These levels are organized into a taxonomy, where the lowest level positions the viewer as a passive observer, removed from moral involvement, while the highest level encourages a reflexive identification with the Other, engaging the viewer as a moral agent. This taxonomy provides an interpretative framework for understanding how different brand narratives shape moral perceptions and influence viewer responses.

In the final stage, I contend that the empathic portrayal of the other in activist brand campaigns underscores the ethical dilemmas in representing vulnerable groups (those who are often marginalized or oppressed). The crucial question is whether these narratives of social justice are genuinely amplified or rather overshadowed by the brand's commercial agenda. However, the solution does not lie simply in imposing specific moral guidelines on advertisers. Instead, the chapter offers a taxonomy of activist brand narratives that serves as an interpretative framework for evaluating representations of the other. This framework seeks to facilitate audience engagement with these portrayals in a way that accurately represents the experiences of vulnerable groups and actively supports substantive social impact.

References

Abad-Santos, A. (2018). *Why the social media boycott over Colin Kaepernick is a win for Nike, Vox*. Vox. https://www.vox.com/2018/9/4/17818148/nike-boycott-kaepernick (Accessed: February 19, 2023).

Ahmed, S. (2013). *The cultural politics of emotion*. New York: Routledge.

Banet-Weiser, S. (2012). *Authentic™: The politics of ambivalence in a brand culture*. New York: New York University Press.

Bartsch, A., & Kloß, A. (2018). Personalized charity advertising. Can personalized prosocial messages promote empathy, attitude change, and helping intentions toward stigmatized social groups? *International Journal of Advertising*, 38(2), 345–363.

Bauman, Z. (2007). *Consuming life*. Cambridge: Polity Press.

Betzler, M. (2019). The relational value of empathy. *International Journal of Philosophical Studies*, 27, 1–26.

Bhargava, V.R., & Bedi, S. (2021). Brand as promise. *Journal of Business Ethics*, 179, 919–936.

Bloom, P. (2016). *Against empathy: The case for rational compassion*. New York: HarperCollins.
Boltanski, L. (1999). *Distant suffering: Morality, media and politics*. Cambridge: Cambridge University Press.
Borgerson, J.L., & Schroeder, J.E. (2002). Ethical issues of global marketing: Avoiding bad faith in visual representation. *European Journal of Marketing*, 36(5/6), 570–594.
Calhoun, C. (1991). Morality, identity, and historical explanation: Charles Taylor on the sources of the self. *Sociological Theory*, 9(2), 232–263.
Carrigan, M., & Attalla, A. (2001). The myth of the ethical consumer – Do ethics matter in purchase behaviour? *Journal of Consumer Marketing*, 18(7), 560–578.
Chen, S. (2023). A counterinsurgent (COIN) framework to defend against consumer activists. *Journal of Brand Management*, 30(4), 275–301. https://doi.org/10.1057/s41262-022-00297-3
Chouliaraki, L. (2006). *The spectatorship of suffering*. London: SAGE Publications.
Chouliaraki, L. (2008). The mediation of suffering and the vision of a cosmopolitan public. *Television & New Media*, 9(5), 371–391.
Chouliaraki, L. (2013). *The ironic spectator: Solidarity in the age of post-Humanitarianism*. Cambridge: Polity Press.
Braun, V., & Clarke, V. (2022). *Thematic analysis*. London: SAGE.
Cohen, J. (2010). *The arc of the moral universe and other essays*. Cambridge, MA: Harvard University Press.
Decety, J. (2021). Why empathy is not a reliable source of information in moral decision making. *Current Directions in Psychological Science*, 30, 425–430.
Decety, J., & Cowell, J. (2015). Empathy, justice, and moral behavior. *AJOB Neuroscience*, 6, 3–14.
Dreher, T. (2009). Listening across difference: Media and multiculturalism beyond the politics of voice. *Continuum, 23*(4), 445–458.
Gangopadhyay, N. (2014). Introduction: Embodiment and empathy, current debates in social cognition. *Topoi*, 33(1), 117–127.
Gillette. (2019). *The Best A Man Can Be*. Retrieved November 13, 2024, from https://gillette.com/en-us/about/the-best-men-can-be
Habegger-Conti, J.L. (2019). Reading the invisible in marjane Satrapi's graphic memoir embroideries. In *Invisibility in visual and material culture* (pp. 149–164). Cham: Springer International Publishing.
Heil, J., & Heil, J.F. (2003). *From an ontological point of view*. Oxford: Oxford University Press.
Hoffmann, M.L. (2000). *Empathy and moral development: Implications for caring and justice*. Cambridge: Cambridge University Press.
Holt, D. (2012). Cultural brand strategy. In *Handbook of marketing strategy*, p. 306. Northampton, MA: Edward Elgar Publishing.
Holt, D., & Cameron, D. (2010). *Cultural strategy: Using innovative ideologies to build breakthrough brands*. Saint Lucia: Oxford University Press.
Honneth, A. (2014). *Disrespect: The normative foundations of critical theory*. Germany: Polity Press.
Hume, D. (1978). *A treatise of human nature*. Oxford: Oxford University Press.
Hunt, S. (2019). The ethics of branding, customer-brand relationships, brand-equity strategy, and branding as a societal institution. *Journal of Business Research*, 95, 408–416.

Husted, B., & Allen, D. (2000). Is it ethical to use ethics as strategy. *Journal of Business Ethics*, 27(1–2), 21–31.
Hutchins, J., & Rodriguez, D.X. (2018). The soft side of branding: leveraging emotional intelligence. *Journal of Business & Industrial Marketing*, 33(1), 117–125
Jacob, P. (2011). The direct-perception model of empathy: a critique. *Review of Philosophy and Psychology*, 2, 519–540.
Jordan, J. (2007). Taking the first step toward a moral action: A review of moral sensitivity measurement across domains. *The Journal of Genetic Psychology: Research and Theory on Human Development, 168*(3), 323–359. https://doi.org/10.3200/GNTP.168.3.323–360
Kamal, M., Qutp, M., & Rashad, Y. (2022). Advertising empathy strategies and their role in influencing the recipient. *International Design Journal*, 12(4), 223–234.
Key, T.M., Keel, A.L., Czaplewski, A.J., & Olson, E.M. (2021). Brand activism change agents: strategic storytelling for impact and authenticity. Journal of Strategic Marketing, 31(7), 1339–1355.
Khamis, S. (2020). *Branding diversity: New advertising and cultural strategies*. New York: Routledge.
Kohlberg, L. (1981). *The philosophy of moral development*. San Francisco: Harper & Row.
Kozinets, R.V., & Jenkins, H. (2022). Consumer movements, brand activism, and the participatory politics of media: A conversation. *Journal of Consumer Culture*, 22(1), 264–282.
Lanzoni, S. (2018). *Empathy: A history*. New Haven, CT: Yale University Press.
Magrì, E., & McQueen, P. (2023). *Critical phenomenology: An introduction*. London: Polity Press.
Martínez García, A.B. (2023). Women activists' strategies of online self-presentation. *AI & Society*, 38(5), 1997–2008.
Matthiesen, N., & Klitmøller, J. (2019). Encountering the stranger: Hannah Arendt and the shortcomings of empathy as a moral compass. *Theory & Psychology*, 29(2), 182–199.
Minocher, X. (2019). Online consumer activism: Challenging companies with Change.org. *New Media & Society*, 21(3), 620–638.
Noddings, N. (2012). The language of care ethics. *Knowledge Quest*, 40(5), 52–57.
Orgad, S., & Gill, R. (2022). *Confidence culture*. Durham, NC: Duke University Press.
Oxley, J.C. (2011). *The moral dimensions of empathy: Limits and applications in ethical theory and practice*. Basingstoke, UK: Palgrave Macmillan.
Papson, S., & Goldman, R. (1998). *Nike culture: The sign of the swoosh*. India: SAGE Publications.
Poulton, M.S. (2005). Organizational storytelling, ethics and morality: How stories frame limits of behavior in organizations. *EJBO: Electronic Journal of Business Ethics and Organization Studies*, 10(2). Retrieved from http://ejbo.jyu.fi
Read, H. (2019). A typology of empathy and its many moral forms. *Philosophy Compass*, 14(10), e12623.
Rest, J.R. (1979). *Development in judging moral issues*. University of Minnesota Press.
Romani, S., Grappi, S., Zarantonello, L., & Bagozzi, R.P. (2015). The revenge of the consumer! How brand moral violations lead to consumer anti-brand activism. *Journal of Brand Management*, 22, 658–672.

Rorty, R. (1989). *Contingency, irony, and solidarity*. Cambridge: Cambridge University Press.
Sartre, J.-P. (1943). *Being and nothingness*. New York: Philosophical Library.
Scheler, M. (2008). *The nature of sympathy*. London: Transaction Publishers.
Shoemaker, D. (2017). Empathy and moral responsibility. In H.L. Maibom (Ed.), *The Routledge handbook of philosophy of empathy* (pp. 242–252). London: Routledge.
Silverstone, R. (2002). Complicity and collusion in the mediation of everyday life. *New Literary History*, 33(4), 761–780.
Silverstone, R. (2013). *Media and morality: On the rise of the mediapolis*. Malden, MA: John Wiley & Sons.
Slote, M. (2007). *The ethics of care and empathy*. London: Routledge.https://doi.org/10.4324/9780203945735
Sobande, F. (2023). *Consuming crisis: Commodifying care and COVID-19*. London: SAGE.
Sobande, F. (2024). *Big brands are watching you: Marketing social justice and digital culture*. Oakland, CA: University of California Press.
Stanley, P. (2020). Unlikely Hikers? activism, Instagram, and the queer mobilities of fat hikers, women hiking alone, and hikers of colour. *Mobilities*, 15(2), 241–256.
Sugden, R. (2002). Beyond sympathy and empathy: Adam Smith's concept of fellow-feeling. *Economics & Philosophy*, 18(1), 63–87.
Szablewska, N., Kamin, T. & Kubacki, K. (2020). Social causes, consumer activism and human rights. In L. Eagle, S. Dahl, P. De Pelsmacker, & C. R. Taylor (Eds.) *SAGE Handbook of Marketing Ethics* (pp. 275–286). London: SAGE.
Thomas, L. (2018, September 4). People are burning their Nike shoes to protest the Colin Kaepernick ad campaign. CNBC. https://www.cnbc.com/2018/09/04/people-burn-their-own-nike-gear-in-response-to-kaepernick-ad.html. Consulted on 13 November 2024.
Vredenburg, J., Kapitan, S., Spry, A., & Kemper, J.A. (2020). Brands taking a stand: Authentic brand activism or woke washing? *Journal of Public Policy & Marketing*, 39(4), 444–460.
Wannow, S., Haupt, M., & Ohlwein, M. (2023). Is brand activism an emotional affair? The role of moral emotions in consumer responses to brand activism. *Journal of Brand Management*. 31(2), 168–192.
Weitzner, D (2022). Patagonia's grand gesture sends the wrong message about ethical capitalism. *The Conversation*. https://web.archive.org/web/20230205081511/https://theconversation.com/patagonias-grand-gesture-sends-the-wrong-message-about-ethical-capitalism-191660
Xie, C., Bagozzi, R., & Grønhaug, K. (2019). The impact of corporate social responsibility on consumer brand advocacy: The role of moral emotions, attitudes, and individual differences. *Journal of Business Research*, 95, 514–530.
Zahavi, D. (2014). *Self and other: Exploring subjectivity, empathy, and shame*. Oxford: Oxford University Press.

3 Digital Dilemmas

Brand Activism in the Age of Algorithmic Influence

The rise of digital media platforms has been pivotal in shaping the ways brands demonstrate their social and environmental commitments while fostering stronger consumer relationships (Carah, 2017; Holt, 2016). This shift is driven by two key factors. First, the growth and diversity of digital advertising avenues have spurred an increase in branded content which now aims not only to sell to but also to engage and entertain audiences (Hardy, 2021). This trend reflects a broader change in marketing strategies, where the focus is as much on creating meaningful connections with consumers as it is on direct selling. Second, social media's role as a catalyst and amplifier in public discourse cannot be overstated. These platforms stir conversations, shape behavioral norms, and facilitate collective action (Gillespie, 2010, p. 347). They have transformed the landscape of public communication, turning individuals from passive recipients of content into active participants in social dialogues. This change of roles is largely due to the democratizing nature of digital media, which empowers users to partake in public discourse (Van Dijck and Poel, 2013).

The integration of digital media into brand-consumer interactions introduces several critical concerns that warrant further examination. While it seems that the alignment between a brand's purpose and consumer values (Williams et al., 2022) might empower consumers, this development also raises significant philosophical questions about the authenticity of such empowerment. One key concern is whether the alignment between brand narratives and consumer values genuinely reflects a commitment to social or political causes, or if it merely functions as a strategic tool for market differentiation. This raises the question: Can ethical commitments maintain their integrity when they are appropriated into marketing frameworks that ultimately serve profit motives?

Furthermore, the use of digital media to promote brand activism introduces a complex dynamic in which algorithm-driven platforms play a pivotal role. The influence of algorithm-driven platforms in shaping perceptions of diversity (Scalvini, 2023) presents significant challenges for brands that aim to cultivate empathetic connections within their campaigns

DOI: 10.4324/9781003105893-3

(Scalvini, 2024). The personalization of social media feeds is significantly influenced by the algorithms that curate and prioritize content. These recommender algorithms are designed to cater to individual user preferences, by analyzing past interactions in order to present content that is presumed to be most engaging or relevant to the user. Individual users are thus more likely to encounter narratives, causes, and stories that align with their existing beliefs, interests, and emotional triggers. These personalized content curators feed users narratives and experiences with which they are predisposed to empathize, and consequently facilitate a form of similarity-based empathy.

Algorithmic recommenders on digital platforms generate a façade of inclusivity, yet they function by narrowing the scope of difference, promoting a homogenized version of society (Scalvini, 2023, p. 10). This process doesn't simply obscure the diversity of alterity; it actively constructs empathy within a framework of similarity, limiting its reach to those who mirror the user's own traits and preferences. Such a structure leads to empathy that is both selective and constrained, reinforcing existing biases rather than challenging them. In the context of brand activism, this dynamic complicates the notion of empathy as a tool for social change. When brands adopt empathy as part of their social responsibility efforts, they enter a space rife with contradictions, as their motives are constantly interrogated by consumers who are increasingly skeptical of the performative nature of such campaigns (Cherrier, 2009). This skepticism is not merely a reaction to perceived inauthenticity but signals a deeper tension in the relationship between commercial interest and moral action. Brands must confront the challenge of aligning their empathy-driven messages with real-world impact, where superficial engagement risks not just failure but a reinforcement of the very systems they claim to critique.

Digital platforms' elevation of certain narratives over others introduces a significant challenge: the creation of an algorithmic interpretive structure that often values stories based on their market appeal rather than the immediacy or severity of the issues they represent. This structure is indicative of some of the ways media representations can mold public empathy and moral engagement with distant tragedies (Boltanski, 1999), underscoring the relationship between visibility, market dynamics, and ethical considerations (Chouliaraki, 2006, 2013; Silverstone, 2002, 2007) a relationship which should be extended to our thinking around algorithmic platforms (Scalvini, 2023).

The prioritization of certain narratives by digital platforms not only creates a skewed perception of social issues but also challenges the authenticity of public empathy. As Boltanski (1999) articulates, the media's portrayal of suffering can significantly influence the public's emotional and moral responses to distant tragedies, shaping which issues receive attention and support. This phenomenon, as further explored by Chouliaraki (2006, 2013) and Silverstone (2002, 2007), reveals a dynamic tension between visibility, marketability, and ethical engagement, where narratives that are more marketable often overshadow those that might be more critical but less appealing to mass audiences. I have suggested that this this ethical examination of media representations and their impact on public empathy must also be applied to algorithm-driven platforms (Scalvini, 2023). These platforms, through their algorithms, exacerbate the creation of a hierarchy of suffering by promoting content that maximizes engagement, often at the expense of genuine empathy toward less visible but equally important issues.

The influence of algorithms on crafting representations directed toward the other adds a layer of complexity to empathy-driven narratives by curating and selecting content based on trends and popularity metrics. These algorithmic mechanisms prioritize content that resonates with individual user preferences and has demonstrated visibility through engagement metrics like likes, shares, and comments. Consequently, the portrayal of the 'Other'—those individuals or groups whose experiences, characteristics, or stories diverge from the user's own—is shaped not purely by the aim of nurturing authentic empathy but by their appeal or prevalence within the digital landscape. This approach to content curation, driven by trendiness rather than a deep commitment to empathy, risks diluting the potential for meaningful connections and understanding between diverse audiences.

In this chapter, I explore the relationship between empathy and moral complacency in the context of activist brand campaigns. This complacency arises as consumers start to see their engagement with brands on social media—such as likes, shares, and comments—as adequate contributions to societal issues. This view is reinforced by algorithm-driven platforms that, while promoting inclusivity, actually lead to a uniformity of content. As a result, these platforms create an environment that appears diverse on the surface but, in reality, undermines true diversity and fosters a misleading sense of universal sameness. A paradox exists within this reality where brand activism's potential for fostering genuine empathy and understanding is juxtaposed with the ease of superficial engagement, raising questions about the depth and authenticity of online moral action.

The research questions this chapter answers are: first, how do individuals discern genuine ethical engagement from performative activism within the context of brand-led social campaigns on digital platforms? This question seeks to examine the critical strategies employed by the public to discern empathy-based representations, particularly in differentiating between campaigns that genuinely align with ethical values and those that exploit these values for marketing purposes. It seeks to understand the criteria or indicators that individuals use to evaluate the authenticity of empathy-based representations within digital brand activism.

Second, what are the ethical implications for marketers and advertisers in crafting empathy-based narratives within digitally mediated activist brand campaigns, considering the risk of commodifying social causes? This question deals with the moral considerations and responsibilities that marketers and advertisers must heed when leveraging empathy to promote social or political causes. It also seeks to explore how these professionals can balance commercial objectives with a genuine commitment to ethical principles in a way that respects the complexity of the issues at hand and avoids trivializing them or exploiting them for brand gain.

Empathetic Representations of the Other

Empathy, while a vital conduit for connecting with and understanding others' experiences, is inherently constrained by our own subjectivities (Overgaard, 2018). This paradoxical nature of empathy—our attempt to grasp someone else's pain through our own emotional lens (Leake, 2011; Paul, 2021)—highlights its dual capacity. On one hand, it draws us nearer to others' experiences, making them more relatable; on the other, it inherently limits our bandwidth of understanding to those who share our perspectives, potentially hindering our ability to grasp others' experiences that are far removed from our own. Therefore, while empathy is a cornerstone of compassion and human connection, it carries limitations and biases that, if unacknowledged, can abet a complacent approach to engaging with the whole spectrum of human experience.

Empathic representation plays a crucial role in inspiring moral action in support of both similar and different Others by bridging the gaps in understanding and nurturing a sense of shared humanity. When individuals encounter representations that resonate with their own experiences or identities—those of the similar other—they are naturally inclined to empathize and act in ways that are supportive and altruistic. This innate response is rooted in the human tendency to care for and protect those with whom one identifies or feels a connection. Literature, art, and media that spotlight shared experiences or emotions can amplify this effect, motivating people to engage in compassionate behaviors and advocate for policies that benefit their immediate communities or groups. When these narratives are shared on social media platforms, the increased visibility further enhances empathy, which can inspire real-world action and support.

Conversely, empathic representation of the different other challenges individuals to step outside their comfort zones and engage with perspectives that diverge from their own. This form of empathy is requisite for social cohesion in increasingly diverse societies. It necessitates a conscious effort to recognize the humanity in those who may live, believe or look differently, thereby promoting actions that are inclusive and aimed at bridging divides. By presenting stories and perspectives of the different Other, representation acts as a powerful tool for dismantling prejudices and expanding one's circle of moral concern. Social media platforms play a critical role in this process, offering a global stage for marginalized voices and facilitating encounters with diverse narratives that can shift perceptions, challenge biases, and mobilize support for causes that transcend individual or group interests.

The transformative power of empathic representation lies in its ability to humanize both the similar and the different other, revealing the intricate web of connections that form the human experience. Through the lens of empathy, individuals are moved to act not just out of self-interest, but out of a profound sense of responsibility toward others. This shift toward empathy-driven moral action has the potential to catalyze societal change, cultivating environments where compassion, justice, and mutual respect flourish. Whether through personal narratives, artistic expression, educational content or branded campaigns, empathic representation serves as a beacon, guiding society toward more ethical and inclusive actions. In the digital age, social media amplifies this impact by enabling the rapid dissemination of empathetic content, engaging a broader audience in dialogue and action, and demonstrating the power of collective empathy to drive positive change in society.

These selected other-related narratives can cultivate a form of empathy that is limited, centered around fragmented stories which might unintentionally overshadow the larger systemic issues at play. From a negative dialectic perspective, the substantial influence of algorithmic-driven platforms reveals the inherent contradictions in online engagement with empathy. This interrogation seeks to dismantle the façade of performative morality and expose the subtle complexities and contradictions in the pursuit of authentic empathy and inclusivity. It challenges the optimistic narrative of seamless progress toward meaningful social change, arguing instead that true transformation requires confronting and working through these contradictions, rather than merely glossing over them with superficial gestures of solidarity.

This perspective demands a critique that resists simplistic resolutions, urging a complex understanding of how empathy and inclusivity can be cultivated within the digital realm. It recognizes the challenging and often contradictory journey toward meaningful societal transformation. In sum, both forms of empathy-based representations face challenges. For similarity-based empathy, there is the risk of reinforcing universal sameness, while for other-directed empathy, the challenge is ensuring that digital representations of the Other are comprehensive and not selective. In this way, transcending moral inaction and complacency is not just about expanding the scope of our empathy; it is about redefining the very nature of ethical engagement in a world where the lines between genuine connection and superficial interaction are increasingly blurred.

Understanding Representations of the Other

Interviews were conducted between 2021 and 2022 with 37 young adults who had been working or studying in the Netherlands for at least 12 months. The interviewees (n = 37) were recruited through a snowballing technique. Interviewees ranged in age from 18 to 25, reflecting the Gen Z demographic, and were predominantly European (n = 54,05%), North American (n = 18,91%), and Asian (n = 16,21%). Of these interviewees, 53.3% identified as male (n = 20), 40% as female (n = 15), and 6.7% opted not to specify their gender (n = 2). The sample can be considered representative of the young adult international community in the Netherlands, encompassing a diverse mix of cultural backgrounds and gender identities. It is noteworthy that between October 2021 and February 2022, the Netherlands observed a stringent lockdown that mandated remote work. Consequently, some interviewees were in their home countries during their respective interviews.

Notwithstanding the varied backgrounds of the interview participants, it is acknowledged that their unique identities and lived experiences may exert influence over their perceptions of activist brand campaigns. Consequently, it is imperative for future inquiries to adopt an intersectional approach to fully comprehend the extent to which individual idiosyncrasies and societal factors shape the perception and appraisal of empathetic responses within such contexts. Saturation was operationalized to be consistent with the research questions (Saunders et al., 2018, p. 1983). By adhering to this operational definition of saturation, the study aimed to achieve a level of data completeness where the findings could be considered both reliable and valid within the context of the research objectives.

Interviews lasted for 45–60 minutes and were semi-structured with open-ended questions. An interview protocol with a list of discussion points was written beforehand (Scalvini, 2023b, Appendix 1). In order to promote a culture of open scientific inquiry, the present study recognizes the value of open data for discouraging research fraud and permitting critical scrutiny. For this reason, the repository of the anonymized transcripts is deposited on Harvard Dataverse (Scalvini, 2023b) in Refi-QDA format. Certainly, the goal is to increase accountability and transparency, and to encourage a new practice of open data in qualitative research by maximizing the value of the interviewees' contributions and increasing diversity in analysis and interpretation.

Utilizing Atlas.ti for data management and coding, this research employed qualitative content analysis with a critical phenomenological perspective, as delineated by Magri and McQueen (2023), to dissect interview transcripts. The analysis proceeded deductively, guided by two main categories: Similarity-Based Empathy and Other-Directed Empathy (Davis, 1996). Through the critical phenomenological lens, the interconnectedness of social identities and their impact on empathic engagement with the Other were examined (Alcoff and Potter, 1993). Furthermore, critical phenomenology facilitates an understanding of how individuals learn to perceive and recognize others within, and in resistance to, hegemonic social backgrounds (Weiss et al., 2019). In the analysis, this critical phenological approach is extended to the influence of digital platforms, which can amplify or distort these intersubjective experiences by shaping the narrative and context in which empathy is conveyed and received (Fuchs, 2014). The inclusion of digital platforms in this analysis underscores the need for a reflective examination of how technology intersects with and influences the empathetic processes and the authentic social engagement they intend to foster.

To ensure the robustness of the coding process, a tripartite methodology (Long et al., 2006) was adopted. The initial phase entailed an assessment of the dataset to identify instances of the two distinct forms of empathy: other-directed and similarity-based. The subsequent phase involved a detailed

Table 3.1 Codebook Categories Applied to Data Analysis

Category	*Operational Definition*	*Coding Instructions*	*Sub-Categories*
Other-Directed Empathy	Involves recognizing and responding to the emotions of others, especially those who are marginalized or vulnerable	Mentions of actions or feelings driven by the needs or emotions of others	• Recognizing emotions of others • Feeling the need to respond or act
		Descriptions of emotional connection without personal gain	• Reference to marginalized or vulnerable individuals • Situational descriptions of other-directed actions
Similarity-Based Empathy	Rooted in the tendency to feel more empathy toward individuals perceived as similar to oneself	Expressions of heightened emotional connection due to shared experiences or characteristics	• Shared experiences or backgrounds • Heightened emotional connection due to similarities
		References to biases in helping or understanding similar individuals	• Biased actions or feelings toward similar individuals • Recognizing oneself in others

examination of the data to ascertain the interviewees' interpretations of empathy. The concluding phase was dedicated to the extraction of concrete examples and occurrences that exemplify the previously identified sub-categories of empathy (see Table 3.1).

Two Strategies: Similarity and Emotional Resonance

This examination revealed two principal narratives accounted by interviewees when engaging with activist brand campaigns on digital platforms. The first strategy harnesses an empathetic approach that seeks to align the audience's experiences with those depicted, thereby fostering a bond through shared values and common ground. The second strategy alternatively endeavors to broaden the moral scope by encouraging the public to extend their empathetic reach to encompass those whose experiences differ markedly from their own. These distinct narrative mechanisms are instrumental in nurturing moral competency and spurring action, with each narrative uniquely tailoring its ethical engagement to resonate effectively with its intended audience.

The two strategies offer distinct pathways toward mobilizing individual and collective agency in moral action. The first strategy, which capitalizes on similarity-based empathy, effectively activates individual agency by making moral dilemmas relatable to personal experiences. By drawing on common ground, this approach personalizes ethical considerations, compelling individuals to reflect on their own values and how these intersect with broader societal issues. This personalization can be a powerful motivator for individual moral action, as it ties the abstract concept of social justice to tangible aspects of the audience's lives, encouraging them to act in ways that are congruent with their personal ethics.

Conversely, the second strategy employs a more inclusive form of empathy and positions itself toward fostering collective agency. By challenging audiences to empathize with experiences vastly different from their own, it expands the moral imagination beyond the confines of personal experience. This broadened perspective is essential for cultivating a sense of collective responsibility and action. It brings to light the interconnectedness of societal issues and the importance of diverse perspectives in addressing them. By elevating stories and voices that may be marginalized or overlooked, this strategy not only amplifies the call for social justice but also reinforces the notion that ethical engagement and moral action are shared endeavors, requiring a collective response.

Seeing Ourselves in Others: The Role of Similarity in Empathy

Similarity-based empathy was consistently echoed throughout the interviewees' narratives. This form of empathy is predicated on the recognition of shared attributes, beliefs or experiences between the consumer and the brand. As consumers encounter brand narratives that reflect their own realities, the emotional resonance is amplified and a sense of self-gratification transpires. An interviewee captured this sentiment in stating, "if you support what they support and you like stand for the same things, you feel connected to them and like, you feel like you trust them and that's really important" (Interview 23, line 289). This alignment is not solely based on surface-level similarities but taps into a deeper, more psychological level of congruence. It is through these perceived shared experiences and values that brands cultivate a powerful emotional bond with their audience.

Expressions of connection through similarity-based empathy often manifest in ways that drive consumers to act, going beyond mere brand preference to active advocacy and defense. Such empathic alignment engenders brand loyalty:

> I think if a brand keeps sending a message that resonates with people. Uh yeah. That activism will definitely help with that brand. And then obviously loyal customers will come along with that as well. Because if it's a message that is continually followed by the same customer, the customer

> will become a stronger follower and more loyal. And yeah they'll sell more to that person.
>
> (Interview 9, line 92)

> You can really see how every brand is striving for diversity and striving to represent everyone and giving every single person really that the brand's speaking to a similar voice.
>
> (Interview 11, line 72)

The expression of similarity-based empathy, as highlighted, not only cements consumer loyalty but also motivates active brand advocacy. This phenomenon occurs as consumers perceive the brand's message and activism to be extensions of their own identity, leading to a protective sentiment toward the brand. Such empathy-driven loyalty illustrates the power of resonant brand messaging to forge deep connections with consumers, as noted in Interview 9. This connection is not superficial; it is rooted in a shared value system and a consistent message that resonates on a personal level, demonstrating the potential of standardized messaging in building strong consumer relationships.

However, the pursuit of diversity and representation, as mentioned in Interview 11, introduces the challenge of balancing genuine inclusivity with the risk of pseudo-individualization. While brands strive to give voice to the diverse experiences and identities of their audience, there lies a thin line between authentically representing such diversity and superficially adopting it as a marketing tactic. The interviewee's observation reflects a consumer awareness of brands' efforts to embody diversity, which, if not carefully managed, could veer into pseudo-individualization, where the attempt to give "every single person… a similar voice" may inadvertently homogenize individual experiences under the guise of inclusivity.

The reflections shared in Interviews 20 and 32 further emphasize the role of similarity-based empathy. When a consumer discovers that a brand shares their viewpoints, it strengthens their loyalty and sense of alignment with that brand. This shared value system is pivotal, as it underpins the consumer's choice, acting as a reflection of their own values and preferences:

> I'm totally happy that the brand that I do love and that I associate myself with has the same opinion as I do. But, if you take into account, for example […] my brand is against something it means that maybe it's not my brand because usually people choose the brands that reflect their own values and preferences.
>
> (Interview 20, line 317)

> People consume products or brands that mirror their own set of values, and therefore a brand should adopt the values of their target audience.
>
> (Interview 32, line 179)

Such alignment is not incidental but fundamental to the consumer-brand relationship, highlighting how essential it is for brands to understand and embody the values of their target audience. Interview 32 reinforces the idea that consumers gravitate toward brands that mirror their value system, suggesting that brands must meticulously curate their values to resonate with their target audience.

The interviewees express satisfaction when a favored brand mirrors their personal opinions, highlighting the significance of value alignment in brand-consumer relationships. This alignment not only reinforces the consumer's positive perception of the brand but also serves as a form of self-affirmation, where the choice of brand becomes an extension of the consumer's identity and moral landscape. However, the excerpts also introduce a critical pivot point: the realization that if a brand takes a stance contrary to the consumer's beliefs on a significant issue, it might lead to a reevaluation of the brand-consumer relationship. This moment of dissonance underscores the conditional nature of brand loyalty, which is contingent upon the brand's continued reflection of the consumer's values and preferences. It suggests that brand loyalty is not just about product satisfaction or aesthetic preference but is deeply entwined with ethical and ideological orientation.

This dynamic suggests that consumers are seeking more than just transactional relationships with brands; they are looking for partnerships with entities that reflect and champion their own values and beliefs. In essence, brand activism becomes a form of social currency, enhancing the brand's appeal to consumers who prioritize ethical considerations in their consumption choices: "Brands that are active in some social issue… if they show a good point of view, they will gain the trust and loyalty of the people that share the same point of view" (Interview 19, line 181). This interviewee expresses appreciation for activist brands because they create communities where people with similar values and experiences come together. This communal space further solidifies the feeling of being understood and being a part of a larger group that "shares similar mindsets" (Interview 19, line 31) such as shared moral values.

Interviewees consider digital platforms to have emerged as powerful tools to amplify this sense of connection. However, one of the interviewees acknowledges a spectrum of engagement among online communities, suggesting that commitment to a cause is not uniform and can be deeply influenced by individual passion and dedication.

> Internet does make us kind of feel like, well online social media presence makes us feel like we're actually being active and like we're actually supporting a cause, whereas it's like latent support, like you're just sitting at home and nothing's really happening. But I do think that there are some people who are very committed and depending on how passionate you are about the topic.
>
> (Interview 27, line 136)

This excerpt reveals the dual nature of social media as both a tool for superficial engagement and a powerful medium. It challenges the binary perception of online activism, inviting a more complex consideration of how digital platforms can both hinder and enhance the pursuit of social justice. The excerpt ultimately calls for a critical reflection on the role of individual agency and passion in determining the authenticity and impact of online support for social causes and highlights the need for a discerning approach to digital activism that prioritizes meaningful action over passive engagement.

The emphasis on digital platforms attests to their indispensable role in shaping activist brand campaigns, underscoring the need for brands to leverage these tools responsibly and effectively in their pursuit of shared values and causes with their consumer base:

> The authenticity of trying to make a change is not there and it's difficult to measure nowadays. And so it's a constant kind of challenge to really perceive what is authentic and activism and what is really, you know, what is really activism in that sense because it has taken all sorts of shapes and forms, than one man, one brand maybe like you know really supporting it. But if they do not use the right platform or means to do so then that is both kind of detrimental for business but also the society.
>
> (Interview 6, line 133)

The choice of medium and method for activism is not neutral; it significantly influences the perception of authenticity and, by extension, the effectiveness of the activism itself. For brands, this choice of the "right platform" is particularly fraught with implications for both their business and their societal impact. Missteps in how activism is pursued or communicated can lead to skepticism about the brand's motives and potentially undermine consumer trust and loyalty. Moreover, inauthentic or poorly executed campaigns can contribute to societal cynicism about corporate social responsibility initiatives, consequently diluting the potential for meaningful change.

When a brand's activism echoes interviewees' sentiments through social media channels, it evokes a profound personal resonance. This is the essence of similarity-based empathy, whereby an individual feels understood and interconnected because their beliefs, feelings or experiences are reflected by the brand. Digital platforms facilitate reciprocal interactions and, within brand activism, this enables consumers to partake actively and engage with the brand's narrative. This occurs due to an individual-centered connection, as one interviewee put it, "it fosters a sense of connection with the brand." (Interview 2, line 109). This connection creates a stronger sense of participation, as it is not just about passive consumption but active engagement, further enhancing the feeling that the brand and the consumer are sharing similar sentiments and values.

To summarize, the essence of similarity-based empathy in brand activism is the profound human inclination to connect with what feels familiar and resonant. This goes beyond superficial attributes and draws on shared values, beliefs, experiences and backgrounds. Brands championing activism, when they tap into this natural tendency, are not just taking a stand; they are building bridges of understanding with their audience. However, digital platforms, by enabling activist brands to craft resonant narratives and fostering interactive dialogues and communities, amplify the feeling of similarity-based empathy. This is because they allow consumers to see their personal values, beliefs and experiences reflected in the brand's activism in the ever-present digital space, creating a strong and consistent sense of mutual connection and understanding.

Emotional Resonance and Understanding the Other

The interviewees' insight into the importance of emotional resonance highlights a key facet of empathy that transcends personal experiences or shared backgrounds. Unlike similarity-based empathy, which is introspective and rooted in commonalities, other-directed empathy centers on the innate human ability to understand, support and emotionally connect with others based on their emotions, needs and vulnerabilities. It references the profound capacity to perceive and recognize the feelings of others, fostering empathy that does not depend on direct personal connections. This distinction points to the broader, more inclusive nature of empathy, showcasing its potential to bridge divides and cultivate compassion across diverse human experiences.

This transcends simple sympathy and moves into a sphere of authentic comprehension. Echoing the sentiments of one interviewee:

> I've watched the Nike 'Dream Crazier' ad frequently. It resonates with me because it doesn't focus on a single individual—it's about inclusion, featuring people with disabilities, women in sports, and others. It represents unity and the collective effort to elevate and embrace inclusiveness.
>
> (Interview 4, line 30)

> I think Nike always managed to stand out or the other because it's just the storytelling is so emotional and the music and everything, the composition of everything is so nice. And I really like seeing stories, like people from backgrounds, they made it up in life and things like that.
>
> (Interview 32, line 24)

This reflection on Nike's 'Dream Crazier' advertisement captures how effectively the campaign promotes unity and inclusiveness through its diverse representations. Instead of focusing on a single protagonist, the ad smartly showcases a wide array of individuals, including people with disabilities and women in sports, thereby illustrating the importance of inclusion and collective endeavor. The Nike television ad, narrated by Colin Kaepernick and titled 'Dream Crazy,' premiered during the NFL's regular season opener on September 6, 2018, which was broadcast on NBC, after which it went viral across the globe via social media.

The repeated engagement with the advertisement via social media highlights thus the significant role these platforms play in making inspiring content readily accessible. Such platforms not only facilitate the easy sharing and revisiting of messages but also empower viewers to spread the campaign's influential narrative further. By adeptly utilizing digital spaces, Nike amplifies its activism, extending its reach and effectively promoting the voices of those often left in the margins. This strategy broadens the ad's impact in addition to reinforcing a powerful narrative of unity and shared struggle, thereby resonating with a global audience.

The interviews revealed a consistent urge across interviewees to respond to perceived injustice or suffering, regardless of personal involvement. This inclination is vividly captured by one participant's reflection:

> Definitely, it links to each other, they speak up for other people and fight for equality and justice with women's marches which is really good, and climate change if it fits into this typical, but they wanna change something and they do something to change it.
>
> (Interview 12, line 49)

> I felt like I related directly, and I felt exposed in a way, so that was interesting to watch.
>
> (Interview 12, line 85)

This interviewee highlights an empathetic reaction defined by a deep personal resonance with the experiences being shared. Other-directed empathy emerges not merely as an emotional response but as a significant catalyst for action. The narratives shared by interviewees frequently pinpointed moments in which the understanding of another's plight or emotional state triggered a strong desire to take action, to offer support or to engage with the cause in meaningful ways. This phenomenon demonstrates the power of empathy to transcend cognitive awareness and actually prompt individuals toward active participation and support, driven solely by the recognition of another's needs or emotions.

Interviewees appreciate brands' potential to use their voice to educate and advocate for what it considers to be the right thing, to utilize other-directed empathy to facilitate broader understanding and compassion among its audience:

> Their brand [Libresse], directly benefits, when you think about it, because the more people talk about vaginas, the more open people are going to be about using pads and perhaps even sharing them with others. You're going

> to like to be more exposed to buying that certain brand, maybe imagine like, I mean this is hypothetical, imagine becomes like really cool to buy a certain brand of pad or something and then you like pass it to your friends and everyone you know is going to end up buying that certain brand of pads. So they're really supporting their products as well.
>
> (Interview 11, line 90)

Other-directed empathy in this specific brand example is cultivated as interviewees become more aware and accepting of the menstruation experiences of others, potentially leading to actions that support and uplift those individuals—such as being more open to discussing menstrual products, sharing them and recommending specific brands that align with these inclusive values. The brand's strategy of intertwining product promotion with social advocacy effectively utilizes its platform to advance its commercial interests as well as engage consumers in a way that promotes empathy and solidarity around menstruation.

Delving deeper into the stories shared, it became clear however that instances of other-directed empathy do not stop at understanding but are about actionable empathy—doing something meaningful driven by a real wish to lessen others' pain or hardship. These activist campaigns can enhance other-directed empathy by using their influence to address and destigmatize social issues, encouraging a broader understanding and acceptance of experiences different from one's own. However, interviewees express a kind of fatigue and overwhelm that stems from the saturation of brands each advocating for different causes:

> It's also about getting bored and overwhelmed because you don't know what brand to like anymore because they all advocate for something. So, you kind of don't specifically link yourself to a brand because they are linked to a cause, because at a certain point you think that there shall be a brand that is a voice for any type of cause.
>
> (Interview 17, line 200)

The interviewee's experience exemplifies a paradox where the abundance of cause-associated branding leads to a form of disengagement as the specificity and uniqueness of brand affiliations become blurred. This highlights a potential downside of brand activism: the proliferation of causes can lead to consumer disengagement, muddying the impact of actions born from empathy. The core of other-directed empathy is rooted in the intrinsic human capability to perceive, validate and deeply resonate with the emotions of others. Therefore, integration of other-directed empathy into the fabric of brand activism becomes particularly powerful within the ecosystem of digital platforms.

It goes without saying that digital platforms offer a vast space for brands to craft and spread stories with the aim of eliciting strong empathetic reactions from their audience. These brand stories are not just about conveying information but are strategically designed to engage the audience's capacity for other-directed empathy. Through compelling storytelling, visual content and interactive experiences, brands strive to connect emotionally with their viewers. This form of engagement seeks to activate the audience's empathy toward distant others, encouraging a deep understanding and emotional response to the characters or causes featured in the narratives. Thus, these brand-driven social campaigns transcend traditional information sharing, leveraging the power of empathy to foster a meaningful connection between the audience and the focal point of the campaign's.

To summarize, other-directed empathy presents a compelling alternative to the typically self-centered stories that predominate in the interactions between consumers and brands. When a brand's message, steeped in other-directed empathy, strikes a chord with a person, it has the potential to establish profound connections, spur authentic actions, and advocate for those who are frequently ignored or sidelined in the wider societal narrative. Harnessing this aspect of empathy allows brands to create significant and impactful relationships, encourage genuine consumer involvement, and support the interests of underrepresented communities.

Ethical Considerations in the Digital Challenges of Brand Activism

The first research question investigates the role of empathy in consumer engagement with brand activism, focusing on the public's ability to discern and assimilate empathetic appeals in the context of brand-led campaigns. In today's era, characterized by the rise of digital affective publics (Papacharissi, 2015), the interaction between collective discourse and individual perceptions has taken on new levels of complexity and importance. This dynamic is further complicated by observations from Han (2015, 2017), who critiques the digital landscape for cultivating a culture steeped in visibility, performance and narcissism, potentially eroding genuine emotional connections and empathy among individuals.

This research question explores the evaluative processes employed by the public when encountering empathy-based representations. It aims to uncover the criteria or mechanisms individuals employ to assess the authenticity of empathy-driven narratives within brand activism. This investigation is crucial in understanding whether digital media, in its quest for visibility and engagement, encourages a depth of empathetic connection or if it inadvertently leads to a superficial engagement with societal issues, prioritizing self-presentation and brand image over meaningful interpersonal connections and collective empathy.

Interviewees frequently underscored brands' capacity to produce narratives that are both based on other-directed empathy and similarity-based empathy, inclusive and beneficial for individuals and the broader society, aligning with the ethos of 'doing good.' Yet, alongside these findings, there was a palpable unease among interviewees about the strategies employed by brands to promote such narratives, the authenticity of the empathetic connections they claim to establish, and whether these strategies are truly ethical or merely opportunistic. This dichotomy indicates the complexity of navigating brand activism when genuine ethical grounding and self-centered justification are increasingly indiscernible.

The longing for inclusivity and empathy motivates interviewees to support brands that seemingly advocate for these values in their campaigns. Interviewees support brands that seem to promote this ideal community through their advertising and marketing. However, they are very aware there may be a gap between this idealistic solidarity and the reality of the brands' commitment to the causes they advocate. This awareness creates a tension between their desire for a community that embodies their ideals and the reality that these brand narratives may be more of a marketing strategy than a true reflection of corporate values. It is this gap between idealism and realism, between the yearning for a perfect community and the questioning of a brand's authenticity, which defines the consumer's relationship with brand activism.

This dynamic suggests that empathy plays a crucial role in navigating the tension between seeking similarity and valuing diversity within the narratives of activist brands. From this tension, two distinct dimensions of moral responsibility emerge: one advocates for a collective, group-oriented approach, and the other emphasizes individual moral judgment. While these two dimensions might initially appear contradictory, they actually illustrate the dilemmas interviewees face in their moral decision-making processes. They must assess whether these narratives—and the brands behind them—genuinely reflect a commitment to care for others and address social issues, or if they merely serve as marketing strategies. This ethics of care, therefore, informs how consumers discern the authenticity of brands' social activism, guiding them toward making moral judgments that align with a holistic understanding of care that encompasses both personal fulfillment and the well-being of others.

This ethics of care is also anchored in the foundational principles of media ethics, especially within the context of digital platforms, where ethical responsibility extends beyond eschewing deceptive practices. It involves cultivating authentic engagement with audiences through narratives that resonate with their values and aspirations. An exploration into the effectiveness of empathetic storytelling within brand activism is necessary to grasp its influence on the perceived genuineness of a brand's social commitments. This determines the trust and credibility an audience places in a brand and is therefore critical for a sustainable and meaningful relationship between digital media representations and public perception.

The second research question explores the ethical landscape that marketers and advertisers must traverse when creating empathy-based narratives, particularly in light of the risks associated with commodifying social causes. This inquiry critically examines the moral obligations and challenges faced by these professionals in utilizing empathy as a tool for promoting social or political issues. It questions how marketers and advertisers can align their commercial goals with a deep-seated commitment to ethical standards and ensure that their approach to sensitive topics is both respectful and conscientious, without reducing social issues to marketing tools for brand benefit.

This normative question seeks to elucidate the ethical duties of marketers and advertisers in deploying empathy-driven narratives in activist brand campaigns, especially in contexts where such campaigns fail to facilitate a genuine shift from empathetic feeling to actionable moral responsibility. Empathy in brand narratives needs to be paired with a coherent and ethical message, as stressed by Khamis (2021), to motivate viewers toward supportive actions but also to move beyond superficial engagement with the cause. Mukherjee and Althuizen (2020) caution against branding strategies that lack moral action, suggesting that without ethical grounding, brand activism risks being perceived as insincere or manipulative.

Furthermore, this research question acknowledges that while brand activism often leverages empathetic storytelling to generate emotional engagement through digital platforms, such empathy can sometimes obscure the deeper political and social structures that underlie injustice, potentially impeding the formulation of effective solutions to systemic problems. The question thus posits that empathy must be integrated with moral principles and values, urging a reevaluation of how empathy is employed within digital brand activism to ensure it contributes materially to social change rather than serve as a superficial appeal to consumer emotions.

Empathy alone is not sufficient to motivate moral action (Singer, 2018)—individuals must also possess the capacity to think about a given situation in a detached manner, allowing them to pause and maintain their own perspective when necessary (Nussbaum, 2001). At the same time, acting morally requires a continuous effort to understand the perspectives of others (Ricoeur, 1992), which can be achieved through engaging with those who hold different views and avoiding the tendency to retreat into familiar and comfortable environments. Therefore, brands seeking to promote social and ethical causes must be mindful of the multifaceted nature of moral action and strive to cultivate a deeper understanding of the issues they aim to address (Couldry, 2012). Digital platforms intensify this imperative as they can generate moralizing discourses that reinforce conformism (Fuchs, 2014); that being said, they also hold the potential to bridge divides by inviting disparate groups into a more comprehensive and inclusive discussion on moral issues (Papacharissi, 2015).

A critical apprehension surrounding the use of an empathy which lacks moral action is its potential to perpetuate and even exacerbate pre-existing power disparities. This use of empathy, ostensibly as a means to understand the Other, can inadvertently become a mechanism for unequal power relations. When an individual endeavors to empathize, they often do so by envisioning themselves in the other's circumstances. However, this imaginative exercise can fall short, particularly and often when the empathizer is positioned in a seat of greater societal privilege or power. Where efforts to understand are compromised by a fundamental disconnect arising from the empathizer's unrecognized privileges, there lies a risk of fostering an empathy that patronizes. This type of empathetic engagement is lacking in grasping the complete reality of the other person's lived experience, consequently solidifying the very hierarchies it seeks to dismantle. This skewed engagement often leads to superficial acknowledgments rather than an equitable dialogue and undermines efforts toward genuine understanding and solidarity.

Empathy filtered through privilege can result in campaigns that, while well-intentioned, ultimately reinforce the status quo and fail to drive intended social change. When brands use empathy in their activism campaigns, it is essential they do so with an awareness of the dynamics of privilege and power. It is not enough just to present the issues on a digital billboard; there must be an effort to educate and facilitate deeper understanding, to encourage action that attempts to rectify the underlying systemic problems, and to involve those who are directly affected by these issues in the creation and dissemination of the campaign. The campaigns must actively and bravely challenge societal hierarchies and promote a form of empathy that is informed, self-reflective and coupled with a clear call to ethical action. Activist campaigns that do otherwise may produce a specious form of advocacy that capitalizes on the visibility of social issues without contributing to meaningful solutions. Such campaigns may garner attention and engender a temporary feeling of solidarity among consumers, but they often lack the substance needed to effect lasting change.

As Fraser argues in *Cannibal Capitalism* (2022), there is a paradox in efforts to cultivate social justice within a capitalist system that frequently drives the very inequalities these efforts aim to resolve. This necessitates utilizing the capitalist framework to nurture an ethics of care that motivates actions and amplifies the agency and voices of affected individuals. Within this scope, morally driven action holds the potential to instigate systemic change. Advertisers and marketers face a moral imperative to progress beyond vague promises of responsible and inclusive conduct and confront the indisputable link between capitalist practices and societal disparities.

In conclusion, this chapter examines how individuals engage with activist brand campaigns that employ empathy and moral appeals through digital platforms. It situates this analysis within the theoretical discourse on advertising and empathy, emphasizing the need for a contextualized approach that accounts for the cultural, social, and technological factors influencing audience responses. The chapter differentiates between forms of empathy, such as similarity-based empathy and other-directed empathy, and analyzes their respective roles in motivating moral action. Particular attention is given to the role of algorithmic mediation, which shapes how these campaigns are distributed and consumed, prioritizing content that aligns with platform logics of engagement and visibility. Accordingly, it recommends a thoughtful integration of empathy with ethical clarity in brand messaging, aiming to inspire audiences toward tangible support for systemic change. This approach ensures that activist campaigns move beyond performative solidarity and make a substantive contribution to social justice.

References

Alcoff, L., & Potter, E. (1993). *Feminist epistemologies*. New York: Routledge.

Boltanski, L. (1999). *Distant suffering: Morality, media and politics*. Cambridge: Cambridge University Press.

Carah, N. (2017). Algorithmic brands: A decade of brand experiments with mobile and social media. *New Media & Society*, 19(3), 384–400.

Cherrier, H. (2009). Anti-consumption discourses and consumer-resistant identities. *Journal of Business Research*, 62(2), 181–190.

Chouliaraki, L. (2006). *The spectatorship of suffering*. London: SAGE Publications.

Chouliaraki, L. (2013). *The ironic spectator: Solidarity in the age of post-humanitarianism*. Cambridge: Polity Press.

Couldry, N. (2012). *Media, society, world: Social theory and digital media practice*. London: Polity Press.

Davis, M.H. (1996). *Empathy: A social psychological approach*. Boulder, CO: Westview Press.

Daykin, J. (2022). *Inclusive marketing: Why representation matters to your customers and your brand*. London: Kogan Page.

Fraser, N. (2022). *Cannibal capitalism: How our system is devouring democracy, care, and the Planet—and what we can do about it*. London and New York: Verso Books.

Fuchs, C. (2014). *Social media: A critical introduction*. London: SAGE.

Gillespie, T. (2010). The politics of 'Platforms'. *New Media & Society*, 12(3), 347–364.

Han, B.-C. (2015). *The burnout society*. Stanford, CA: Stanford University Press.

Han, B.-C. (2017). *Psychopolitics: Neoliberalism and new technologies of power*. London: Verso Books.

Hardy, J. (2021). *Branded content: The fateful merging of media and marketing*. London: Routledge.

Holt, D. (2016). Branding in the age of social media. *Harvard Business Review*, 94(3), 40–50.

Khamis, S. (2021). Branding diversity: New advertising and cultural strategies. London: Routledge.

Leake, E.W. (2011). *In the words of another: On the promises and paradoxes of rhetorics of empathy*. Louisville, KY: University of Louisville.

Long, T., Pantaléon, N., Bruant, G., & d'Arripe-Longueville, F. (2006). A qualitative study of moral reasoning of young elite athletes. *The Sport Psychologist*, 20(3), 330–347.

Magri', E. & McQueen, D. (2023). *Phenomenological approaches to ethics and information technology*. The Stanford Encyclopedia of Philosophy.

Mukherjee, S., & Althuizen, N. (2020). Brand activism: Does courting controversy help or hurt a brand? *International Journal of Research in Marketing*, 37(4), 772–788.

Nussbaum, M.C. (2001). *Upheavals of thought: The intelligence of emotions*. Cambridge: Cambridge University Press.

Overgaard, S. (2018). What is empathy?. In *Husserl's phenomenology of intersubjectivity* (pp. 178–192). London: Routledge.

Papacharissi, Z. (2015). *Affective publics: Sentiment, technology, and politics*. Oxford: Oxford University Press.

Paul, L.A. (2021). The paradox of empathy. *Episteme*, 18(3), 347–366.

Ricoeur, P. (1992). *Oneself as another*. Chicago: University of Chicago Press.

Saunders, B., Sim, J., Kingstone, T., Baker, S., Waterfield, J., Bartlam, B., Burroughs, H., & Jinks, C. (2018). Saturation in qualitative research: Exploring its conceptualization and operationalization. *Quality & Quantity*, 52, 1893–1907.

Scalvini, M. (2023). Making sense of responsibility: A semio-ethic perspective on TikTok's algorithmic pluralism. *Social Media + Society*, 9(2), 1–14.

Scalvini, M. (2023b). Brand activism and GenZ, https://doi.org/10.7910/DVN/6HNVQ8, Harvard Dataverse, V1.

Scalvini, M. (2024). Empathy and ethics in brand activism: Balancing engagement and responsibility. *New Media & Society*. Advance online publication. https://doi.org/10.1177/14614448241278344

Silverstone, R. (2002). Complicity and collusion in the mediation of everyday life. *New Literary History*, 33(4), 761–780.

Silverstone, R. (2007). *Media and morality: On the rise of the mediapolis*. Polity.

Singer, P. (2018). *The expanding circle: Ethics, evolution, and moral progress*. Princeton University Press.

Thevenin, B. (2022). *Making media matter: Critical literacy, popular culture, and creative production*. New York: Taylor & Francis.

Van Dijck, J., & Poell, T. (2013). Understanding social media logic. *Media and Communication*, 1(1), 2–14.

Weiss, G., Murphy, A.V., & Salamon, G. (Eds.). (2019). *50 Concepts for a critical phenomenology*. Evanston, IL: Northwestern University Press.

Williams, P., Escalas, J.E., & Morningstar, A. (2022). Conceptualizing brand purpose and considering its implications for consumer eudaimonic well-being. *Journal of Consumer Psychology*, 32(4), 699–723.

4 Aligning Corporate Morality

The Challenges of Brand Activism and Consumer Trust

In this book so far, I have argued that the politics of empathy adopted by brand activism can be used to promote social justice and transformational change (Dean, 2019). For example, an advertisement that foregrounds the experiences of marginalized communities or raises awareness about social issues (Khamis, 2023) can evoke empathy in viewers and encourage them to take action (Pollay, 2000). By using empathy to create a sense of shared humanity, these advertisements can help to build bridges across cultural and social divides and engender greater understanding and compassion. However, a politics of empathy can also depoliticize social movements by centering individual narratives, thereby diverting attention from the structural dynamics and power relations that underpin these struggles.

The strategic deployment of empathy within brand activism carries significant normative implications. First, by selectively highlighting specific issues and framing them through emotionally charged narratives, such activism can shape societal norms and values. This selective focus may lead to a disproportionate emphasis on individual suffering, potentially obscuring the underlying systemic issues and depoliticizing broader social movements. Second, the politics of empathy inherent in brand activism can influence our perceptions of who is deemed worthy of empathy and protection (Ahmed, 2014). By strategically associating certain groups or causes with specific emotions, brands can subtly manipulate our moral judgments and actions, potentially reinforcing existing societal biases or even generating new ones.

However, this analysis may present a somewhat limited view, portraying consumers as passive recipients of emotional manipulation rather than active agents with their own motivations and interpretations (Gabriel and Lang, 2015; McCracken, 1989). Consumers are not merely passive recipients of empathetic appeals, but actively seek out and engage with narratives that resonate with their values and desires (Kozinets, 2002; Schau et al., 2009). This active participation complicates the notion of manipulation, as it implies a degree of agency and complicity on the part of consumers (Baudrillard, 1998). Following this line of thought, the strategic use of brand activism as a means of transformational change raises questions that extend beyond the

DOI: 10.4324/9781003105893-4

mere manipulation of emotions. It prompts us to consider whether marketers genuinely believe in the causes they champion and whether consumers truly believe in these campaigns, or if both parties are simply playing their roles in a larger social game.

While marketers may aim to influence consumers through branding (Arvidsson, 2006; Holt, 2004), the way that consumers perceive and interact with brands is ultimately dependent on their own beliefs, experiences and values (Klein, 2000; Thompson and Arsel, 2004). Thus, consumers play an important role in shaping the success and impact of brand activism as their responses can ultimately determine whether a campaign is effective or not (Camarrotta et al., 2023, Verlegh, 2024). However, it must be noted that this is a paradoxical condition. On the one hand, people have the power to challenge these branded narratives and demand more meaningful action for social change. On the other hand, they may perpetuate the fantasy by accepting superficial or tokenistic efforts by brands and not fully engaging with the underlying issues of social injustice and inequality.

In this chapter, I utilize a thematic analysis to analyze interviews conducted with both marketers and consumers, in order to answer the following questions: How do brand activism campaigns balance moral education with genuine efforts to address the roots of societal issues, and what impact does this have on consumer engagement? What are the ethical implications when brands adopt political stances within their advertising and how does this influence consumer perception, brand authenticity, and the potential for backlash? How can activist brands cultivate a comprehensive understanding of social justice to ensure their activism aligns with societal values and transcends mere transactional morality?

Exploring Marketers' and Consumers' Perspectives on Brand Activism

The initial dataset comprises insights gleaned from interviews with 10 brand managers in the consumer goods industry, based in London, Amsterdam/Rotterdam, and Zurich. These professionals shared their perspectives on brand activism, emphasizing their rationale and viewpoints on the subject. It is important to note that while the discussions were open and based on publicly available information, no sensitive data was disclosed during these conversations. The cases of brands discussed in the interviews were drawn from publicly accessible sources Prior to publication, explicit authorization was obtained from each interviewee for the inclusion of their excerpts in this chapter, ensuring respect for their privacy and professional boundaries.

The study strictly maintained the anonymity and confidentiality of the participants by adopting practices such as anonymizing identifiable information and ensuring that discussions did not veer into confidential or proprietary territory. To further uphold the confidentiality of the interviewees, excerpts included in this book have been carefully edited to omit specific brand names directly managed by the participants. This editing process was undertaken with the dual aim of preserving the professional integrity of the interviewees and ensuring that no confidential information was inadvertently disclosed. The research protocol was designed to avoid questions that might elicit sensitive information, thereby safeguarding the confidentiality of the participants and their organizations throughout the study.

The second dataset was compiled from interviews conducted in 2020 with 48 young adults who were either working (55% of participants) or studying (45% of participants) in the Netherlands. This group was initially accessed through snowball sampling from a base group of five Dutch students in Rotterdam. The participants, aged between 18 and 25 (with an average age of 21.5), predominantly come from the European Union (52.27% including non-Dutch nationals from the Czech Republic, Germany, Spain and Latvia) and international regions (36.36%, including Australia, Canada, Georgia, Russia, Mauritius and Vietnam), with 43% identifying as male and 57% as female. This demographic mix mirrors the diverse young adult international community in the Netherlands. Notably, during the interview period, the Netherlands was under a strict lockdown, leading to some participants being interviewed remotely from their home countries.

Interviews ranged from 45 to 60 minutes, adhering to a semi-structured format with discussions revolving around a predetermined set of topics (Scalvini, 2024, Appendix 1). With a commitment to promoting open scientific inquiry, this study prioritizes open data practices to prevent research fraud and encourage thorough scrutiny, enhancing transparency and accountability. The anonymized consumer interview transcripts are available on the Harvard Dataverse (Scalvini, 2024) in Refi-QDA format. This initiative is intended to maximize the contributions of the participants and broaden the scope for diverse analyses and interpretations, advancing the practice of open data in qualitative research.

For data management, this study utilized Atlas.ti to aid in the application of thematic analysis, as outlined by Braun and Clarke (2022). The analytic process was deductive, guided by the categories defined within the theoretical framework. This approach facilitated a systematic analysis of the data, which is utilized in subsequent sections to elucidate the relationship between brand activism strategies and consumer perceptions.

Operationalization

In examining brand activism, this study has operationalized key concepts through three themes to evaluate and compare the perspectives of brand managers and young adults. These themes—Corporate-Social Alignment, Ideological Engagements and Consumer Expectations—provided a structured approach to understand the interrelationship between corporate intentions and consumer reactions within the realm of brand activism.

The first theme **Corporate-Social Alignment** centers on the congruence between a brand's outward moral education and its internal operations, values and practices. It examines whether there is harmony or discord between what a brand professes to support in terms of societal issues and how it behaves behind the scenes—such as in its corporate practices, employee relations and supply chain ethics. This theme is fundamentally about the internal-external coherence of a brand's actions and messages. It is concerned with the depth to which a brand integrates its social activism with its core business operations and the genuine commitment it shows toward the causes it supports. The focus here is on identifying whether a brand's activism is embedded in its organizational fabric and ethos or if there is a disconnect that could lead to a lack of trust among consumers about the brand's involvement in social issues.

The second theme **Ideological Engagements**, on the other hand, dives into the dynamics between a brand's public adoption of political or social stances and the perceptions and reactions it evokes among consumers. It explores how a brand's chosen causes and the manner in which it communicates and advocates for these causes resonate with or alienate its consumer segments. This theme is more about the external interaction between the brand's public-facing activism and the consumer base's values, beliefs and expectations. It scrutinizes how consumers interpret and respond to a brand's ideological positioning, the value they attribute to these engagements based on their alignment with personal beliefs, and the consequent support or backlash the brand receives. Here, the emphasis is on the consumer-brand relationship through the lens of shared or conflicting ideologies.

The third theme **Consumer Expectations** shifts the focus toward the expectations that consumers and society at large have regarding the role of brands in contributing to social justice and societal values. Specifically, this theme explores how brands can meet consumer expectations through their campaigns, ensuring that their efforts are not only visible but deeply rooted in genuine, impactful actions that reflect a commitment to societal progress. The theme also considers the implications of such engagements for a brand's legitimacy in the eyes of consumers, assessing how consumer intentions influence purchasing decisions and loyalty. This evaluation extends to the wider social contract between brands and the public, scrutinizing how brands can actively participate in and shape discussions and actions related to justice and equity.

Corporate-Social Alignment

The first theme addresses the relationship between a brand's stated commitment to social causes and its concrete actions. It explores how brands reconcile moral advocacy with meaningful efforts to address societal challenges at their roots. This theme explores the ramifications of such alignment (or lack thereof) on engaging consumers. Consumers may feel that they are 'doing their part' potentially reducing their motivation to engage in more substantial activism or demand broader systemic change. For example, the approach taken by a vegetarian hamburger brand to promote minor, sustainable lifestyle changes—like opting for plant-based meats—exemplifies a unique blend of moral education with brand activism. This strategy does not just advocate for sustainability through corporate actions; it actively aims to reshape consumer habits and societal consumption patterns. The brand's effort to influence individual choices and broader cultural practices highlights a commitment to sustainability that extends beyond traditional corporate responsibility.

However, this focus on individual action may inadvertently foster complacency (Chapter 1). If consumers believe that simply switching to plant-based burgers is enough to address climate change, they may become less inclined to demand broader systemic changes, such as stricter regulations on industrial farming or greater investment in renewable energy. The brand's message, while well-intentioned, may inadvertently create a false sense of progress, leading consumers to believe that the problem is being adequately addressed through their individual choices. This can ultimately hinder the push for more comprehensive solutions and delay the necessary transformation of our food systems.

By encouraging such shifts, the brand not only contributes to environmental sustainability but also educates its consumers on the importance of their daily choices in promoting a more sustainable world. This method demonstrates how brands can use their influence to drive genuine change, making a significant impact on both individual behavior and societal norms:

> Our goal is to inspire people to make small, impactful changes in their daily routines, such as choosing plant-based meats instead of animal meat once or twice a day. We believe these minor adjustments can significantly contribute to sustainability while allowing people to maintain their cultural traditions. Our focus is not just on highlighting the problems but providing solutions and encouraging a shift towards more sustainable choices. By promoting this message, we aim to engage consumers with our brand, differentiating ourselves in a market full of active brands, each with its unique message. For us at the [name brand] emphasizing these sustainable choices is at the heart of our mission.
>
> (Manager 1, line 72)

Unfortunately, the habit of brands copying each other's successful moves reduces what could be powerful acts of societal engagement to mere marketing tactics. It is a game of waiting and watching, with brands hesitant to make the first move toward real change, preferring instead to tread in the footsteps of others. This behavior not only questions the depth of their commitment to change but also highlights a broader issue about creativity and originality in brand activism. However, the interviewee quoted below recognizes a group of brands driven by a true desire to make a difference. This recognition serves as a reminder that not all efforts are lost to marketing strategies, and that genuine intent to contribute positively to society still exists:

> Honestly, I see some brands out there kind of copying what works for others because they think, "Hey, that's a solid marketing move." It's like everyone's looking around—some at the government, others at consumers—wondering who's going to make the first move to shake things up. But the truth is, we can be that change. I mean, there are loads of us in the brand world who genuinely want to do the right thing. It's like we're all part of this big community trying to push for something better. Take vegetarian options, for example. If what's out there isn't cutting it for me, chances are, it's not working for others either. So, why not step up and offer something that could make more people consider going vegetarian? It's all about not waiting on the sidelines for someone else to step in. We've got the power to make those changes ourselves.
>
> (Manager 1, lines 144–145)

The emphasis on providing vegetarian options transcends dietary preferences and signals a broader expectation for brands to embrace ethical considerations and actively participate in shaping societal values. This perspective encourages brands to move beyond conventional commercial roles and adopt a principled approach that prioritizes authentic social contributions over simply reacting to market trends.

However, framing this issue solely as a choice between conforming to established norms with conservative approaches or embracing moral leadership through innovative practices presents a limited and potentially problematic perspective. It implies that innovation is inherently good and established norms are inherently bad, which is an oversimplification. A more sophisticated approach would recognize that both innovation and established norms can be valuable tools for brands seeking to make a positive impact.

Instead, the interviewee's insights bring up a key challenge for brand activism: How can companies balance staying true to themselves and making a real difference in the world, all while working within the limits of the current business environment? This approach acknowledges that brand activism exists on a spectrum, with varying degrees of risk and reward. It also emphasizes the importance of thoughtful consideration and strategic decision-making when choosing how to engage with social issues.

This moral inflection point underscores the ethical responsibility of brands to not only engage in societal conversations but also to actively drive meaningful change. It challenges them to reconsider their role and impact by undertaking initiatives that address fundamental societal values and challenges. However, it's important to note that this expectation for brands to take a leading role in social change can be seen as arising from both ethical considerations and the dynamics of the capitalist market.

While there is a moral imperative for brands to act responsibly and contribute to the betterment of society, it's also true that in today's market, consumers increasingly expect brands to take a stand on social issues and align their actions with their values. This creates a market-driven incentive for brands to innovate and differentiate themselves by demonstrating their commitment to social responsibility.

Therefore, pressure on brands to innovate and take the lead on social issues arises from a dynamic interaction between ethical responsibilities and market demands. While some may criticize this as simply a capitalist imperative, it's important to recognize that these two factors are not mutually exclusive. Brands can, and should, strive to create a positive impact on society while also pursuing their business goals. The key is to ensure that their actions are authentic, transparent, and genuinely aligned with their stated values.

For instance, the initiative to combat food waste illustrates brand activism's capacity to align with and amplify consumers' increasing awareness of environmental and social issues. Similar to the plant-based meat example above, this approach goes beyond traditional corporate responsibility, actively seeking to instigate societal change by prompting consumers to adopt more sustainable practices in their daily lives:

> You know, a lot of folks aren't aware that throwing away food ends up being one of the biggest contributors to greenhouse gases. It's a massive problem for climate change. Imagine, if instead of tossing out what we don't eat, we used up everything we bought. It sounds simple, but it could make a huge difference—not just saving the planet but saving families a bunch of money and making sure they're getting all the nutrition they need. That's exactly why we've been on a mission to tackle food waste since 2018, doing it the [name brand]'s way. Given we're a staple in so many homes around the world, we've got a real shot at making a difference. We're trying to get the word out there, telling folks to use what they've got instead of just shrugging it off as 'Oh, it's just one carrot, what's the harm?' But here's the thing: 60% of food waste happens right at home, and most people don't even realize they're contributing to climate change every time they throw food away. We're here to help change that, even if it's with something small.
>
> (Manager 2, line 66)

However, this raises critical questions about the depth and sincerity of such campaigns. While encouraging consumers to make environmentally friendly choices represents a positive step, it also shifts the onus of responsibility onto individuals, potentially absolving corporations of systemic and much more catastrophic contributions to environmental degradation. This strategy, although well-intentioned, warrants scrutiny to ensure that it is not a veneer of genuine corporate commitment to sustainability, but rather, that it is part of a bigger, more comprehensive strategy to address the sources of environmental damage.

The two examples above reflect the strategy adopted by marketers specifically targeting Western markets. It is also interesting to consider how certain management teams react to the tension between a brand's global ethical responsibilities and its alignment with local cultural norms and practices. For example, rebranding a skin whitening product involves addressing the tension between cultural preferences and global ethical concerns, particularly in relation to beauty norms and the implications thereof:

> At the end of the day, respecting different cultures is key, even if some practices might not align with Western values. It's really a case-by-case situation. Take, for example, skin whitening creams in India, a staple in not just India but across Asia and Southeast Asia. These products are everywhere, from every major brand like L'Oreal to P&G. While in the West, there's considerable controversy over promoting fair skin in post-colonial countries, in places like India, skin whitening is a cultural norm, widely accepted by the vast majority. Despite this product being a top seller, we decided to rebrand it. This decision was risky; renaming a popular brand could mean a significant financial hit due to potential loss of recognition and sales. Yet, we felt it was necessary to address the broader implications and align better with global sensitivities.
>
> (Manager 3, line 54)

This situation underscores the brand's effort to manage the tension between acknowledging cultural differences and responding to ethical concerns. By modifying its branding to be more sensitive to global criticisms of skin whitening practices, which are often associated with racial and colonial undertones, the brand acknowledges the complexities of operating in a diverse global market. While these products may be culturally normalized in certain markets, such as India, they also face significant ethical controversies in the West, particularly due to post-colonial sensitivities toward beauty standards.

However, it's important to note that the claim of skin whitening being a widely accepted cultural norm in India is a contested one. Within India's highly caste-based system, skin tone has historically served as a marker of social status, with lighter skin often associated with higher castes and privilege. This has led to a complex relationship with skin whitening products, where their use can be seen as both a personal preference and a reflection of deeply ingrained societal biases. Therefore, the brand's decision to continue marketing these products in India, even with modified branding, may be viewed as perpetuating harmful stereotypes and reinforcing discriminatory practices.

In this first theme, consumer engagement is codified by perceptions of the brand's overall integrity and commitment to social causes. Consumers, however, often regard these efforts with a critical eye, trying to distinguish which initiatives are genuine and which are performative. This critical perspective assesses the depth of corporate commitment to social and environmental causes and the role of brand narratives in shaping consumer behavior and societal norms in meaningful ways. In my interviews with young adults, a notable example of this is the distrust expressed toward H&M's "conscious" line where, despite the brand's attempt to market itself as environmentally friendly, consumers question the real impact of these initiatives. This disbelief reflects a broader trend of young consumers demanding transparency and meaningfully transformed business practices, not just labels with an "eco-friendly" stamp. The perception that these efforts are more about brand success than environmental protection shows the need for companies to substantiate their claims with tangible actions that align with their marketed values:

> Um, I think it's good. I think it's good that brands are becoming more aware that they should try to be more ethical and that consumers are sort of demanding them to be more ethical. Um, I don't know sometimes how ethical it is, even though they're branding that they're very ethical. So, for example, I know H&M and they have this conscious line that's supposed to be way better for the environment. However, I think it's still really, I don't think it's actually that much of a change, but they just sort of brand it in a different way. Yeah. So then I think it's still bad, even though they're trying to make it look good, it's still kind of bad. But I think the companies that are making a change, I think that's good because it's you know, if that's something that they just do, then why not?.
>
> (Consumer 9, line 33)

> Uh. A lot of brands are doing that. Not sure they're doing that or just claiming they're doing that. But then I think for the big corporations, big organizations such as the like the big multinational like Shell or Alibaba or Amazon, they always have their PR team to work on something that they're great for the society or environment, those kinds of pieces. I mean, of course, if there is such a big corporation, they must have done something good for the society or for the environment. But then is that enough or.? Yeah.
>
> (Consumer 22, line 113)

This sentiment extends into the domain of food consumption, where the preference for organic and non-genetically modified foods among young adults highlights the difficulty of making informed choices amid competing claims of health and sustainability in the marketplace. Their efforts to make informed decisions about their food consumption reflect a broader desire for authenticity in product offerings, making it imperative for corporate activism to be transparent and genuine, allowing brands to build trust and credibility among consumers:

> Well, I try to eat mostly organic food if I can find them. But obviously when you buy something, there's not a hundred percent chance that, you know, what's inside it because a lot of markets, shops, whatever you want to call them. They do genetically modified food, such as potatoes and corn and stuff to make it look more appealing and like to make it look like it's healthy and good, or maybe even add color and stuff. So I wouldn't say I'm necessarily picky, like, although I am, but like I said, you never know what you put in your mouth.
>
> (Consumer 4, line 37)

This lack of trust toward the authenticity of 'healthy' or 'natural' food labels reflects a general mistrust in corporate claims, revealing a disconnect between consumer expectations and actual corporate practices. It stresses the critical role of clear, verifiable information in building consumer trust and loyalty, especially in a time when the authenticity of brand activism is under intense scrutiny.

These interviewees' call for enhanced transparency and meaningful practice also represents a demand for brands to craft more relatable and persuasive stories about their activism efforts, stories which do not fabricate alignment with the values and expectations of their audience. However, this call emerges within a context where navigating the tension between advocating for social causes and steering clear of contentious political stances is essential.

For instance, an initiative like building schools, while inherently positive, can draw suspicion if perceived as a branding exercise rather than an act of social responsibility. Brands need to support positive developments, but do so in a manner that shows they are driven by a genuine desire to effect change, rather than a desire to self-promote:

> Well, I think, you know, people like to see positive developments more than they like to see negative developments. So, you know, any way of showing that you are really supporting positive developments, not only in the short term, but also in the long term. For instance, let's say you're building a school, and your company has a big name on top of this school. Of course, it's a bit 'on the nose' and people start seeing like "Ahh man, this f*cking company, they're using their name again," see? But, I think people will see like, "Hey, these people are actually trying to make a difference.
>
> (Consumer 34, line 127)

This complexity shows that brand activism must reflect the brand's core identity and values to be experienced as legitimate and resonant with young consumers. It should avoid superficial gestures and focus on real change.

Doubt around attempts to exploit social movements, like posting a black square on Instagram to protest police racism after the death of George Floyd in 2020, highlights the tight rope brands must walk. Consumers can quickly tell genuine advocacy from surface-level solidarity, often criticizing brands for either not speaking up or engaging in what is seen as performative activism. This puts brands in a tough spot, requiring them to show support without coming across as being insincere or trying to save face:

> Yeah. Because there were a lot of people who, when they heard a brand did post that black square on Instagram, they were like, oh, well, either that seems insincere. So, they weren't buying because they were like, oh, it's performative activism. Or when they didn't post, they were like, oh, you silent on this issue. So it was kind of like a damned if you do, damned if you don't.
>
> (Consumer 44, line 87)

The real challenge for brands is making their activism efforts a core part of their identity to assure their engagement with societal issues is not just for show but aligns with their values. This demands more than symbolic gestures; it calls for actual contributions to social causes, building stronger connections with consumers and enhancing the brand's credibility.

Younger generations' active environmental consciousness and their demand for significant corporate action have led to a growing expectation for brands to not only contribute but also take the lead in creating a sustainable future. This tension between individual actions to protect the environment and the environmental initiatives undertaken by corporations as a whole highlights a broader conversation about the roles and responsibilities of various actors in addressing global challenges. To clarify, this tension is not between individual people and individual corporations, but rather between the cumulative impact of individual choices (such as recycling, reducing consumption, etc.) and the broader systemic changes that need to be made by corporations and governments to address the root causes of environmental problems:

> Honestly, I think it's good that the younger generations really care about the Earth and are so active about it. For, example my niece, she uses a metal straw instead of plastic straws that she brings everywhere with her. She's about like 14 years old and I think it's cute and I really like that it is a proactive way to make this world a better world and make sure we can live on this Earth for a longer time than if we would go through the way we are doing now. But I personally think that there are also like other initiatives to pursue a better world one day and I honestly think that like big brands or yeah companies with big, huge impacts should be more active about this. Because they are causing the problem and consumers are just passively buying if you know what I mean.
>
> (Manager 1, line 148)

Venturing into political activism is a bold move for brands, as it comes with its own set of controversies. While taking a stand on social issues can enhance a brand's appeal to a more conscious consumer base, it also risks alienating segments of the market. Thus, the decision-making in brand activism often involves pitting social contribution against the potential for controversy:

> Some of the biggest names in the industry have started taking a political stance. Brands stand up for what they believe in to fulfill their responsibility towards society and attract the right kind of audience. Today's generation is more aware of social issues and the importance of taking a stand. Hence, they would rather be loyal customers of companies making political statements rather than the ones who remain neutral.
>
> (Consumer 12, line 89)

The effectiveness of brand activism hinges on the alignment—or misalignment—between corporate efforts and actions that meet the expectations of a society that values transparency, authenticity, and meaningful action. The interviewed consumers, who are young adults aged 18–25, evaluate corporate initiatives with a discerning eye for their actual impact, looking beyond marketing campaigns for evidence of real, beneficial change. This demographic's scrutiny challenges brands to resist aligning superficially with societal expectations and instead integrate these values into their core operations and philosophy. The brand's activism must reflect its foundational principles and demonstrate a long-term commitment to social betterment, proving its activism is not fleeting or disingenuous.

It's important to note that this demographic (post-millenials) has grown up in an era of heightened awareness of social and environmental issues, and they are often more critical of corporate actions that they perceive as insincere or performative. This is in line with the broader literature on children, young people, and marketing awareness, which highlights how younger generations are increasingly lack of trust in traditional marketing tactics and demand greater transparency and accountability from brands.

The comparison between brand managers' strategies and the expectations of young adults reveals a fundamental disjunction: skepticism toward the sincerity of corporate efforts to address systemic injustices. While brand managers articulate strategies that ostensibly integrate values such as sustainability into corporate narratives, young adults often interpret these initiatives as performative, calling into question whether such claims represent substantive commitments or calculated appeals to consumer sentiment. This tension exposes an epistemological problem: whose perspective determines the legitimacy of activism, and what constitutes "authenticity" in a media-saturated environment?

From an ethical standpoint, brand activism foregrounds unresolved questions about the nature of corporate responsibility in relation to social justice.

The discourse suggests that corporations have moved beyond merely marketing values to curating their visibility as moral actors. Yet, young adults interviewed in this context challenge the sufficiency of visibility, arguing for transparency that not only discloses intentions but actively transforms structures of power. In demanding alignment between corporate activism and broader ethical imperatives, they do not seek consistency alone but a willingness to disrupt the asymmetries that sustain corporate influence.

The ethical interrogation of brand activism, therefore, must go beyond assessing the integrity of individual campaigns. It requires a reframing of the relationship between corporate actions and their legitimizing frameworks. Rather than aiming to satisfy societal expectations, brands must confront the structural limitations of aligning activism with profitability. This is not a question of building stronger ethical foundations but of critically reimagining how brands define social impact within the constraints of their institutional logic. Without this reimagination, brand activism risks functioning as a mechanism for reproducing, rather than addressing, the very inequalities it claims to oppose.

Ideological Engagement

The second theme interrogates the role of brands in shaping societal discourse by examining how their public positions influence consumer perceptions and modes of engagement. The expectation for brands to align with the ideologies and demands of their audience is not simply a strategic necessity but a manifestation of a broader societal insistence on purpose-driven corporate behavior. Yet, this dynamic raises a paradoxical question: do the values and beliefs that brands communicate reflect genuine commitments, or does the audience's demand for purpose inadvertently commodify morality, reducing ethical engagement to a market-driven exchange of expectations and symbolic gestures?

In a climate of increasing consumer suspicion toward corporate motives, the challenge for brands lies not in their ability to advocate for social causes, but in their capacity to demonstrate genuine commitment:

> My background's in activism and campaigning, mostly with NGOs. We always saw three major players: governments with their legislative power, civil society with people power, albeit limited, and businesses with their massive messaging power and budgets. Much larger budgets in business compared to civil society, right? Transitioning to a corporate role was a leap for me. I was curious how a brand could act as a true activist, pushing for progressive change. Reflecting on my time with activist brands, it's clear, brands wield incredible communication power.
>
> (Manager, 9, lines 35–36)

This excerpt not only contributes to our understanding of the strategic role of co-opting civil society in shaping public discourse but also prompts a reflection on the ideological motivation that guides such endeavors. From a critical perspective, this strategy exposes a tension between the pursuit of commercial success and the responsibility for brands to wield their communicative power to contribute meaningfully to societal discourse. How effective a brand's engagement in social advocacy, therefore, becomes a litmus test for brands' transcendence of traditional marketing tactics and embodiment of the values they espouse, all amidst growing consumer scrutiny and demands for real, impactful change.

The brand's energetic shift from passive to active engagement in socio-political discourse requires a critical extraction of brand intentions from their narratives. The notion that brands, primarily driven by profit motives, can sincerely participate in meaningful societal change without commodifying social issues is put up for debate:

> I recall Benetton's campaigns vividly, featuring images like starving children or a man dying of AIDS, which, frankly, had nothing to do with their clothing line. Their approach was to signal awareness of global issues, effectively broadening their brand's appeal. It was a clever strategy, albeit with a hint of manipulation, suggesting that their engagement with these issues wasn't entirely driven by altruism but also by the brand-building potential such provocative imagery held. Benetton became a major brand through this tactic, which blurs the line between raising awareness and leveraging serious issues for brand visibility. Ben & Jerry's has also faced internal conflicts, especially within Unilever, their parent company to find a right mix between social activism and brand identity.
>
> (Manager 5, line 7)

The accounts of Benetton's and Ben & Jerry's ventures into brand activism capture the specific challenges brands encounter when integrating social issues into their narratives.

By embedding their brand identity within the broader fabric of social and political discourse, these companies position themselves at the intersection of marketing and activism. However, this convergence complicates the boundaries between societal engagement and strategic self-interest, blurring the distinction between commitments to social improvement and efforts to enhance brand visibility.

The increasing expectation for brands to engage with ideological stances reframes brand activism as a process of ideological construction rather than alignment. This process positions brand activism not as an ethical extension of corporate identity but as a mechanism for organizing public expectations around social engagement within the constraints of market imperatives. Performativity, rather than being an occasional misstep, operates as a foundational logic, turning social values into assets to be leveraged. Far from transcending traditional marketing, this framework integrates brand activism more thoroughly into corporate strategies, questioning whether ethical engagement can exist outside its instrumental role in sustaining corporate legitimacy.

This perspective demands an examination of whether brands are truly committed to the values they promote or if these narratives are a strategic façade to attract a socially conscious consumer base. Interviewee 6 adds a layer of complexity to the discussion by focusing on the importance of maintaining brand integrity when engaging in activism:

> People often say it's just a marketing gimmick when a brand strays too far from its roots or hops on the bandwagon just because it's the trend. You've got to be cautious about what you stand for as a brand. You can't drift too far from what the brand has always been about. Nowadays, many brands are starting with a focus on social or political issues before even creating their products. It's an interesting shift, similar to how [Name's brand] began in the 19th century, aiming to provide nutritious food for everyone. This approach to sustainability and nutrition shows genuine intent since it's all about addressing societal needs right from the start.
>
> (Manager 6, lines 44–45)

This interviewee points to a necessarily fundamental link between brands' social initiatives and their foundational principles and purpose. When campaigns stray from these founding values, it risks splintering consumer trust. The example of a food brand founded to provide the basic societal need of nutrition illustrates how marketing can quite straightforwardly make responsible and conscious contributions. However, this point raises concerns about the potential for commercial interests to dilute sincere social engagement: even a food brand can engage in malpractices for the sake of profit. However, if brands can align their activism with their core mission and values, they can uphold their credibility in a market that values ethical and principled action.

In this second theme, engagement is more directly tied to how well the brand's specific ideological positions align with those of its consumers. Thus, the young adults I interviewed scrutinize brand actions, especially symbolic gestures such as Blackout Tuesday's black square posts supporting BLM, approaching them with a critical and skeptical perspective. They question whether these gestures stem from a genuine position of anti-racism or whether brands are caving to societal pressure:

> So the protests, I stand behind, as long as they're peaceful. And because a lot of the time they do get out of hand, but I, I am a believer that if you want change, you have to go get it. But putting a black picture on Instagram is not, for me at least, not the best way to do that. I think a lot of people, the majority of people, in my opinion, could change their profile picture to a black picture to go along with the so-called hype train. Because they were

> either scared of not doing it and getting criticised by friends, or they were doing it to get loved by their friends and hearing Oh, so good that you're doing it. I think there's better ways to do it than just put a picture.
>
> (Consumer 46, line 159)

This viewpoint implores substantive, impactful activism, urging brands to go beyond symbolic gestures in favor of concrete actions. The following interview excerpts raise questions about the effectiveness of boycotts and online activism against global corporations, suggesting that while individual contributions might seem small, they embody a conscious engagement with corporate behavior.

> I think they only work when a brand is, or when a corporation isn't big enough. So, with Facebook, Facebook is way too big. Like Amazon as well, it's way too big to try and break it down so in that sense I really don't think it's working. But for smaller brands. A lot of people don't need it. I think it's a lot easier to hurt him, hurt the brand, one where when we're boycotting it or making hashtags like that. But Facebook and Amazon, it's kind of useless almost, but I feel like even though I think it brings peace to me when I do it. You know, I know, just one person won't do anything about it, but I feel like I'm contributing to something when I do it, even though it doesn't really make sense.
>
> (Consumer 2, line 78)

This standpoint holds that more than simple gestures are needed, questioning the real impact of boycotting or engaging online with massive corporations like Facebook or Amazon. However, it also acknowledged that while such efforts might seem small or even futile, given the scale of these entities, individual contributions reflect a true internal dedication to holding corporations accountable.

> I think as one individual, I don't think I'm creating much change. But I think that if I would say, well, nobody is doing it, so therefore I won't do it. I feel like that's also a really bad way to start and I maybe if I or someone would do the same and, you know, if I can try out a certain product that is sustainable or you know that I know is doing good. And then I'm trying it out for someone else so I can help someone get into that journey a lot faster so, I don't think as a person I'm doing a lot, but I can do a lot if I continue to be like this. Instead of laying back and wanting someone else to solve the issue for me.
>
> (Consumer 2, line 141)

The interviews reflect a realistic yet hopeful view of activism's power and limitations. Conceding that actions against larger corporations might not directly result in visible change, individuals nonetheless value their participation as part of a collective effort to advocate for better corporate practices. This sentiment emphasizes that even small, personal choices, such as supporting sustainable brands, play a crucial role in driving broader societal changes.

When exploring whether brands should adopt more political stances to resonate with consumers, two contrasting viewpoints were presented. The case of Patagonia illustrates a brand leveraging its platform to champion environmental issues through direct political messaging, exemplifying how activism can galvanize community support and drive societal change:

> I think Patagonia is a political brand, especially I have seen an advertisement where they had labels that said "Vote these assholes out", which shows that this brand has a strong political standing against people who are in power and do ignore climate change. And they're not afraid to show it and share it with their followers and other people. So I would say that yes, they are a political brand.
>
> (Consumer 14, line 119)

Conversely, there was apprehension of the implications of brands engaging in politics, underscoring potential pitfalls such as customer confusion and adverse reactions. This cautionary view signals the complexities of intertwining brand identity with political advocacy, spotlighting the unpredictable nature of consumer responses and the potentially negative impact on brand reputation and sales:

> I think a brand being political would just cause more confusion and problems because, you're never really certain about how people will react to these kinds of situations and how this might influence the brand and their sales in the future, because it could either negatively affect them or it could also positively affect them if everyone else also agrees with their ideas and thoughts, but I don't personally think that it's right to mix fashion with politics.
>
> (Consumer 14, line 115)

Concerns were specifically noted about the appropriateness of blending politics with industries like fashion, indicating some reluctance to see brands adopt overt political positions and questioning whether such actions align with the core values and expectations of their audience.

Through these interviews with young consumers, a key insight emerges: both personal decisions and collective actions are foundational to effective activism. Individual efforts, when pooled together, can create a ripple effect, encouraging companies to adopt more responsible practices. These micro-efforts not only challenge brands to work genuinely toward societal betterment but also highlight the importance of each person's role in advocating for change, reinforcing the idea that collective action starts with individual choices.

Within the theme of Ideological Engagement, the divergence between brand strategies and the perceptions of young adults raises important questions about the production and mediation of meaning in brand activism. Brand managers often gravitate toward causes that align with hegemonic values, selecting issues such as anti-racism or environmentalism that resonate broadly within the cultural mainstream. This approach, while appearing ideologically neutral, operates as a form of symbolic management that minimizes political risk while maximizing emotional resonance. It functions less as an act of advocacy and more as a negotiation of visibility—deciding which struggles are legible within the moral economy of the brand.

The young adults interviewed present a distinct perspective, emphasizing the material consequences and systemic implications of corporate initiatives. They approach symbolic actions—such as the widely criticized posting of a black square during Blackout Tuesday—with skepticism, recognizing these gestures as performative rather than transformative. This skepticism reflects a broader expectation for brands, demanding structural interventions that produce measurable social change. Their evaluation of corporate actions underscores the need for brands to demonstrate accountability and effect meaningful societal contributions.

Most of the interviewees remain acutely aware of the asymmetrical power dynamics between consumers and corporations. While they recognize the potential of collective pressure to nudge brands toward more ethical practices, they also articulate a pragmatic understanding of the limitations of consumer influence within entrenched corporate structures. This duality—between the desire for impactful activism and the acknowledgment of systemic constraints—raises pressing questions about the mechanisms through which consumer advocacy can disrupt, rather than reinforce, the market-driven frameworks of brand activism.

In conclusion, brand managers strive to construct narratives that position their brands as advocates for social change, closely aligned with prevalent moral and ideological values. Yet, young adults scrutinize these efforts, demanding tangible impact and sincerity. Successful brand narratives should reflect societal ideologies and embody a genuine commitment to improving society. It is an essential requirement for brands to internalize ethical principles amid societal expectations and consumer evaluations. The core challenge is ensuring brand actions, and not just their narratives, resonate with societal values and meet consumer expectations.

Consumer Expectations

This theme concerns how a brand's involvement in social issues affects what consumers think of it and how they act toward it, based on whether their actions line up with what people expect and value in society. When brands actively contribute to making things better in society, people take notice—it can shape whether they stick by the brand or not. This connection between what a brand does for society and how people respond to it is key. If a brand is seen doing good and matching up with societal values, it earns more respect and loyalty from consumers. Essentially, this theme explores the idea that how a brand acts in the bigger picture can directly influence whether people decide to buy from it, support it or recommend it to others.

For instance, I discussed the case of Ben & Jerry's with many of the interviewees, their responses demonstrating the influence of a brand that commits to social issues with strong conviction. As part of a multinational corporation, Ben & Jerry's has managed to retain its distinct identity, leveraging its origins and steadfast values to engage with social causes:

> Taking a stand always comes with its risks, and Ben & Jerry's really embodies that unapologetic stance. A bit of history for you: Ben & Jerry's wasn't always under Unilever; it started as its own thing. And even now, as part of Unilever, it operates pretty independently. Their management team's out in Vermont, where it all began, and there's no global Ben & Jerry's team here in Europe—it's all run from the States. This setup lets them keep a bit of distance from the broader Unilever mindset, focusing less on mass appeal and more on connecting with their audience directly. In my view, this independence gives them an edge. They're not just another brand; they're a brand with a mission, ready to stand by their values without the fear of alienating the mainstream.
>
> (Manager 3, lines 112–113)

Adopting an operational mindset akin to Ben & Jerry's is not without its challenges and potential pitfalls. As clarified by Interviewees 4 and 5, political stances can lead to a brand alienating segments of its market who may not share the same values or perspectives on these social issues. This risk is further compounded in the global market, where cultural and societal norms vary significantly across borders, making a one-size-fits-all approach to brand activism potentially problematic.

Specifically, Interviewee 4 points out there is a fine line between leveraging activism as a core part of a brand's identity and using it as a marketing tactic or a form of risk management. This distinction is crucial, as the latter may lead to perplexity among consumers, diluting the brand's message and potentially undermining its efforts to contribute meaningfully to societal discourse and progress:

> I often see it as more optimistic than sincere. Many companies seize the opportunity to advocate for certain causes, seeing it as a way to increase market share or as a necessary risk management strategy. For instance, the widespread corporate support for Black Lives Matter raises questions

> about whether these companies genuinely address minority issues internally. It's a classic case of talking the talk without walking the walk. But there are also companies that truly care and take action, using their business to make the world a better place. When companies live up to their values and embed them into their brand activism, it becomes a powerful tool, potentially more influential than NGOs in some cases.
>
> (Manager 4, lines 42–43)

When a company loudly supports social movements like Black Lives Matter but fails to make meaningful changes within its own walls, consumers pay attention and begin to ask questions ridden with doubt. However, there are brands that truly practice what they preach and entrench their values deeply into their business operations. This genuine approach not only earns consumer trust but also demonstrates that a brand's commitment to social issues can influence consumer choices just as powerfully, if not more so, than traditional non-profit efforts.

The interviewee's insight into how some brands may use support for social causes primarily as a marketing tool suggests a more transactional approach to social advocacy, aimed more at boosting sales than making a real impact. This strategy, though it might initially draw consumer interest or meet immediate demands, carries the risk of harming a brand's reputation over time. If consumers perceive these efforts as insincere or merely opportunistic, the damage to trust and brand image could outweigh any short-term gains, suggesting that genuine commitment to social causes is not just ethical but also essential for sustaining long-term brand loyalty and respect.

Interviewee 5 lays out the dual-edged nature of brand activism: on one side, the risk of perceived inauthenticity threatens corporate legitimacy, and on the other, the impact of genuine, values-driven activism is profound:

> Brand activism isn't just about taking a stand; it's about doing so strategically. You need to think carefully about how your message might be received, because you don't want to turn off a big part of your customer base. This means being especially cautious when talking about sensitive topics like politics, religion, or culture—these areas can be really complicated and easily misunderstood. The trick is to find a balance: speak out in a way that's meaningful but doesn't go too far, so you can make a difference without pushing people away.
>
> (Interview 5, line 13)

The caution against alienating large segments of the consumer base underscores the risks inherent in brand activism. The balance mentioned here is not just about avoiding negative backlash; it is about genuinely contributing to the conversation in a way that is meaningful yet mindful of the brand's diverse audience. This excerpt touches on a fundamental tension within brand activism: the need to take a stand on important issues without alienating wide swathes of consumers.

A key objective of this theme is to examine whether the values championed by activist brands align with consumer expectations. For example, one interviewee discusses the conscious effort to avoid brands associated with negative practices, such as Chick-fil-A and McDonald's, due to their controversial histories. However, this ethical stance softens when it comes to purchasing Christmas products, where the focus shifts to the joy of the recipient rather than the moral, health or political implications of the product:

> I would say that, of course, I try at least to not buy things that I know are really bad. I try not to. Yeah. If a company I don't know is hard, the Chick fil A issue, for instance, and in America, if I would, I would not buy from there. And also McDonald's I try to avoid as it's just a really big brand. And I know that it's been a bit controversial over the times, so I would not buy from them as much as possible. But yeah, when coming down to Christmas products, I don't really pay much attention to any moral or health or political reasons as I rather just see something that I think the other person would enjoy.
>
> (Consumer 3, line 100)

This shows a conflict consumers face: aligning their individual beliefs with the social norms and expectations prevalent during culturally significant times, such as holidays. Navigating consumerism within the framework of normative expectations is demonstrably complex: individual choices are influenced by a multitude of factors, including societal norms, personal values, spending power and the specific context of the purchase.

Another interviewee gave Patagonia top marks for its focus on making clothes that last. This praise came after watching some of the brand's videos on social media which spotlight Patagonia's strong commitment to sustainability:

> I think it's actually a really good video to, yeah, to make people stop for a second and realize that, OK. Yeah. Is that really, am I just buying and spending money because there's a discount or am I really getting a coat because I really need a new coat for instance. Yeah…
>
> And what do you think about the Patagonia brand?
>
> (Interviewer)

> I do know it. I don't own any clothing myself, but I do think it's a, it's a nice brand. Their products look nice. And now after the video, I also realized that they're long lasting clothes, which is also something that is really important. And I might actually get myself something from Patagonia later on when I need it (laughs).
>
> (Interview 3, line 75)

The positive feedback suggests that when a brand transparently communicates its values and aligns its actions with those values, it resonates well with even unfamiliar consumers. This approach of engaging consumers with meaningful content and high-quality products illustrates a successful strategy in brand activism. It not only informs but also inspires consumers to support brands that reflect their own ethical and environmental concerns. This case demonstrates the impact and importance of authentic engagement in strengthening consumer trust and loyalty toward a brand.

The interviewees also expressed a growing interest in adopting more ethical consumption practices, such as buying from local farmers and reducing their environmental footprint. This change indicates a consideration of their purchasing decisions' ecological ramifications:

> I buy what's easily accessible to me at the moment, but I try to minimize. I try to throw away less of that and I'm actually slowly going into buying from for example, fruits and vegetables and slowly growing into buying it from local farmers instead of large corporations. Even though it's not like, I feel like I can't do it in one click. I think it's a process and I really don't shame anyone or anything for not doing it. It's just a personal thing.
>
> (Interview 2, line 57)

Acknowledging the transition to ethical consumerism as a journey directly connects to the role brands can play in supporting consumers on this journey, not just through advocating for change, but by providing products, services and education that align with these evolving values, making the transition more accessible.

This excerpt from Interview 6 offers a compelling perspective on consumer power and responsibility in the context of brand activism and corporate behavior. The interviewee suggests that the most effective method to counter corporate practices that are unethical or misleading—such as greenwashing—is through informed consumer choices,

> The best way to fight them is to show it with your purchases. Where you do not buy their products anymore, and work at those companies yourself and change things internally. Because like this, the same people will be working at these companies, who will not change things. Also looking at the way so many companies use greenwashing nowadays. So, the best way is to look at yourself with this, and not buy those products again.
>
> (Interview 6, line 51)

By choosing not to purchase products from companies that do not align with environmental standards, consumers send a clear message regarding the values they support. Moreover, the interviewee proposes an even more proactive approach: working within these companies to drive change from the inside.

This suggestion acknowledges a critical insight—that without a change in the people who make and execute decisions, transformative shifts in corporate practices are unlikely.

The mention of greenwashing specifically highlights a growing concern among consumers about the authenticity of companies' environmental claims. This practice, where companies exaggerate or fabricate their sustainability efforts, has made consumers increasingly skeptical of corporate messaging. The interviewee's advice to "look at yourself with this" invokes the role of personal responsibility and agency in fostering corporate accountability. It suggests that individual actions, both as consumers and potentially as employees, can collectively influence corporate strategies toward more genuine sustainability efforts.

Brands hold significant influence in shaping societal norms and consumer behaviors through their marketing strategies. However, this power is not unilateral; it is continually contested and reshaped by the collective voice of consumers, particularly young adults, who leverage their purchasing decisions and public discourse to hold brands accountable. This dynamic tension underscores the shift toward a more democratized relationship between corporations and consumers, where the latter wield considerable influence over the former's reputation and legitimacy. As consumers increasingly prioritize ethical practices and sustainability, they challenge brands to realign their actions with societal expectations, thereby reshaping the power dynamics within the marketplace.

Acting for the Good of Others, or at Least Believing So

The first research question examines how marketers manage the tension between providing moral education and making substantive efforts to address the underlying causes of societal issues. The analysis reveals that while social-corporate alignment can be a powerful tool for engaging consumers (Carrigan and Attalla, 2001), there is a critical need to extend beyond consumer engagement to address societal challenges effectively. This strategy influences consumer engagement by cultivating a connection and commitment to the cause (Vogel, 2007), yet it also raises concerns about the potential for consumer complacency (Chapter 1). When brand activist campaigns are not complemented by actionable solutions, there is a risk of creating a sense of moral fulfillment without necessitating further action or reflection from the consumer. However, the interviewed consumers often view these activist campaigns as profit-driven endeavors, questioning the sincerity and effectiveness of such initiatives.

During the interviews, brand managers discussed brand activism as a moral imperative to promote social change. This strategy generates a sense of distrust among consumers, they are conscious, agentic and critical of meaningless moralism. The contrast between marketers framing brand activism as a moral imperative and consumers' disbelief about its sincerity reveals a fundamental disconnect in how brand activism is perceived. This divergence reflects a broader dialogue on the role of empathy in brand narratives (Chapter 1 and 2)—where consumers seek not just emotional resonance but also concrete, impactful actions that address societal injustices. This gap between corporate intentions and consumer expectations highlights the challenge brands face in convincingly integrating social issues into their identity without being perceived as capitalizing on these issues merely for profit.

This contradiction has important ethical implications as the moral imagination situates public action within a framework of private skepticism (Zizek, 1997). It separates the cultural dimension of empathy, which focuses on self-expressive narratives that demonstrate commitment to vulnerable others (Chapter 2 and 3)), from the political dimension of empathy (Chapter 1), which emphasizes understanding human vulnerability as a matter of injustice (Chouliaraki, 2006, 2013). Advertisers must integrate the cultural dimension of empathy with a political commitment to justice, ensuring that consumer engagement transcends distrust.

The second research question explores the impact of brand activism on consumer doubt and the perceived sincerity of corporate commitments (Carrigan and Attalla, 2001; Mohr et al., 2001). Brand managers' strategies and perspectives on brand activism, designed to weave societal values into the fabric of their brand narratives (Holt, 2004; McAlexander et al., 2002), often aim to resonate with or even reshape prevailing societal ideologies. These efforts, encompassing sustainability and ethical practices (Brown and Dacin, 1997; Handelman and Arnold, 1999), reflect a strategic intent to align brands with contemporary societal movements and consumer expectations. However, the reception of these strategies by interviewed young adults reveals a contradiction. This demographic, often approaching corporate commitments with a critical perspective, regularly questions the sincerity and actual impact of these initiatives (Chatzidakis et al., 2007; Varadarajan and Menon, 1988), exhibiting lack of trust toward actions viewed as merely performative. This observation points to a misalignment between the objectives of brand managers and the type of engagement consumers seek, raising broader questions about the credibility and effectiveness of brand activism (Obermiller and Spangenber, 1998).

When brand activism is perceived as credible and resonant with the values of young adults, it strengthens corporate legitimacy, cultivating trust and loyalty within this demographic. Meaningful engagement in social and environmental causes, evidenced by transparent and substantive actions, aligns with the priorities of young adults (Bhagwat et al., 2020), creating a stronger connection with the brand. This alignment not only enhances the brand's public image but also drives consumer advocacy and support (Cammarota et al., 2023), as young consumers are more inclined to engage with and promote brands that align with their values and visions for social progress.

Conversely, when there is a clear misalignment between brand managers' activism efforts and the expectations of young adults, the implications for corporate credibility can be detrimental (Schroeder and Borgerson, 2018). Perceived inauthenticity or superficial engagement in societal issues can lead to distrust and disengagement from the brand (Vredenburg et al., 2020). In an era where consumers, particularly young adults, increasingly seek brands that contribute meaningfully to societal betterment, the failure to meet these expectations can result in a loss of consumer support and damage to the brand's reputation (Carrigan and Attalla, 2001). This perplexity may extend beyond individual brands and influence wider perceptions of corporate activism (Wagner et al., 2009, Bhagwat et al., 2020).

The final question explores how activist brands can cultivate a broader, more inclusive approach to justice, ensuring their activism authentically mirrors societal values and transcends transactional motivations. Brands wielding significant influence have the capacity to educate their audience on social justice matters when they utilize a comprehensive justice lexicon (Rawls, 1973). Through purposeful campaigns, content marketing, and social media engagement (Chapter 3), brands can demonstrate a capacity for self-reflection and critical awareness, fostering brand reflexivity (Chapter 2). This not only elevates awareness of social issues but empowers consumers to make informed, values-driven choices, cultivating a more conscientious consumer culture (Micheletti, 2003).

To address the challenges effectively, marketers must refine their approach to empathy, understanding its bounds while integrating well-founded arguments for justice (Fraser, 1990). This adjustment requires a shift toward reflection on and active engagement with social issues (Sobande, 2024; Khamis, 2022), moving beyond the use of emotive narratives as the sole driver for moral action (Chapters 1 and 2). While brand activism serves to highlight social causes (Cammarotta et al., 2024; Verlegh, 2024), it should act as a supplement to, rather than a replacement for, genuine social advocacy (Banet-Weiser, 2012). Building a richer discourse on justice necessitates brands' active involvement with diverse voices, particularly those from underrepresented communities (Sobande, 2019) to avoid the selective empathy (Chapter 1). By forming partnerships with NGOs, community organizations, and dedicated activists, brands can bolster the legitimacy of their initiatives, ensuring they genuinely reflect the nature of social challenges and resonate with the lived experiences of those affected. This collaborative approach not only enhances the credibility and effectiveness of the brand's actions but also deepens their audience's comprehension and engagement.

The gap between brand managers' intentions and consumers' perceptions underscores the urgent need for a strategic overhaul in brand activism (Vredenburg, 2020). Brands must transcend virtue signaling to engage in practices that genuinely reflect ethical and societal commitments (Mukherjee and Althuizen, 2020; Sobande, 2019). This shift necessitates a dedication to establishing and maintaining legitimacy, with brands embodying the change they advocate for in their foundational operations (Handelman and Arnold, 1999; Suchman, 1995). Looking forward, the focus should be on developing engagement strategies and practices that are transparent and accountable, ensuring that brand activism is in harmony with the values and expectations of a socially aware audience.

In summarizing the insights from this chapter, it is evident that the primary challenge for brand activism extends beyond leveraging empathy to captivate audiences—it's about ensuring such engagement leads to substantial societal change. The analysis reveals activist brands are evaluated for their depth and sincerity in tackling systemic problems, rather than merely amplifying social causes for brand advantage. This scenario calls for a shift from a transactional model of brand engagement, where social initiatives predominantly serve brand image, to a more heartfelt approach that emphasizes social impact. Hence, brands are encouraged to embrace moral reflexivity, where their activism transcends marketing tactics to become a genuine effort in contributing to social betterment. Such an approach demands brands to not just superficially engage but to adopt a role that genuinely mirrors their commitment to effecting positive societal shifts.

References

Ahmed, S. (2014). *The cultural politics of emotion* (2nd ed.). Edinburgh: Edinburgh University Press.

Arvidsson, A. (2006). *Brands: Meaning and value in media culture*. London: Routledge.

Banet-Weiser, S. (2012). *Authentic (TM): The politics of ambivalence in a brand culture*. New York: New York University Press. https://doi.org/10.18574/nyu/9780814739372.001.0001

Batra, R., & Keller, K.L. (2016). Integrating marketing communications: New findings, new lessons, and new ideas. *Journal of Marketing*, 80(6), 122–145. https://doi.org/10.1509/jm.15.0419

Baudrillard, J. (1998). *Consumer society: Myths and structures*. London: Sage Publications.

Belk, R.W., & McCracken, G. (1989). Culture and consumption: New approaches to the symbolic character of consumer goods and activities. *Journal of Marketing*, 53(3), 125. https://doi.org/10.2307/1251348

Bhagwat, Y., Warren, N.L., Beck, J.T., & Watson IV, G.F. (2020). Corporate sociopolitical activism and firm value. *Journal of Marketing*, 84(5), 1–21. https://doi.org/10.1177/0022242920937000

Boltanski, L. (1999). *Cambridge cultural social studies: Distant suffering: Morality, media and politics* (G.D. Burchell, Trans.). Cambridge: Cambridge University Press.

Brown, T.J., & Dacin, P.A. (1997). The company and the product: Corporate associations and consumer product responses. *Journal of Marketing*, 61(1), 68–84. https://doi.org/10.1177/002224299706100106

Cammarota, A., D'Arco, M., Marino, V., & Resciniti, R. (2023). Brand activism: A literature review and future research agenda. *International Journal of Consumer Studies*, 47(1), 1–15. https://doi.org/10.1111/ijcs.12967

Carrigan, M., & Attalla, A. (2001). The myth of the ethical consumer – Do ethics matter in purchase behaviour? *The Journal of Consumer Marketing*, 18(7), 560–578. https://doi.org/10.1108/07363760110410263

Chatzidakis, A., Hibbert, S., & Smith, A. (2007). Why people don't take their concerns about fair trade to the supermarket: The role of neutralization. *Journal of Business Ethics*, 74(1), 89–100.

Chouliaraki, L. (2006). *The spectatorship of suffering*. London: SAGE Publications.

Chouliaraki, L. (2013). *The ironic spectator: Solidarity in the age of post-humanitarianism* (1st ed.). Cambridge: Polity Press.

Dean, J. (2019). *Publicity's secret: How technoculture capitalizes on democracy*. New York: Cornell University Press.

Fraser, N. (1990). Rethinking the public sphere: A contribution to the critique of actually existing democracy. *Social Text*, 25/26, 56. https://doi.org/10.2307/466240

Gabriel, Y., & Lang, T. (2015). *The unmanageable consumer*. London: SAGE Publications.

Goldman, R.L., & Papson, S. (1996). *Sign wars: The cluttered landscape of advertising*. New York: Guilford Publications.

Handelman, J.M., & Arnold, S.J. (1999). The role of marketing actions with a social dimension: Appeals to the institutional environment. *Journal of Marketing*, 63(3), 33–48. https://doi.org/10.1177/002224299906300303

Holt, D.B. (2004). *How brands become icons: The principles of cultural branding*. Boston: Harvard Business Review Press.

Illouz, E. (2013). *Cold intimacies: The making of emotional capitalism* (1st ed.). Cambridge: Polity Press.

Khamis, S. (2023). *Branding diversity: New advertising and cultural strategies*. New York: Routledge.

Klein, N. (2000). *No LOGO*. London: Picador.

Kozinets, R.V. (2002). The field behind the screen: Using netnography for marketing research in online communities. *JMR, Journal of Marketing Research*, 39(1), 61–72. https://doi.org/10.1509/jmkr.39.1.61.18935

McAlexander, J.H., Schouten, J.W., & Koenig, H.F. (2002). Building brand community. *Journal of Marketing*, 66(1), 38–54. https://doi.org/10.1509/jmkg.66.1.38.18451

McCracken, G. (1989). Culture and consumption: A theoretical account of the structure and movement of the cultural meaning of consumer goods. *Journal of Consumer Research*, 16(1), 71–84. https://doi.org/10.1086/209204

Micheletti, M. (Ed.). (2003). *Political virtue and shopping: Individuals, consumerism, and collective action*. Basingstoke, UK: Palgrave Macmillan.

Mohr, L.A., Webb, D.J., & Harris, K.E. (2001). Do consumers expect companies to be socially responsible? The impact of corporate social responsibility on buying behavior. *The Journal of Consumer Affairs*, 35(1), 45–72. https://doi.org/10.1111/j.1745-6606.2001.tb00102.x

Mukherjee, S., & Althuizen, N. (2020). Brand activism: Does courting controversy help or hurt a brand? *International Journal of Research in Marketing*, 37(4), 772–788. https://doi.org/10.1016/j.ijresmar.2020.02.008

Nussbaum, M.C. (2010). *Upheavals of thought: The intelligence of emotions*. Cambridge: Cambridge University Press.

Obermiller, C., & Spangenberg, E.R. (1998). Development of a scale to measure consumer skepticism toward advertising. *Journal of Consumer Psychology: The Official Journal of the Society for Consumer Psychology*, 7(2), 159–186. https://doi.org/10.1207/s15327663jcp0702_03
Papacharissi, Z.A. (2013). *A private sphere: Democracy in a digital age* (1st ed.). Cambridge: Polity Press.
Pollay, R.W. (2000). The distorted mirror: Reflections on the unintended consequences of advertising. *Advertising and Society Review*, 1(1). https://doi.org/10.1353/asr.2000.0012
Rawls, J. (1973). *Theory of justice*. Oxford: Oxford University Press.
Scalvini, M. (2024). Consumer perspectives on brand activism and ethical choices: Navigating shopping habits. *Sustainability, and Social Responsibility*, https://doi.org/10.7910/DVN/M73TX5, Harvard Dataverse, V1.
Schau, H.J., Muñiz, A.M. Jr, & Arnould, E.J. (2009). How brand community practices create value. *Journal of Marketing*, 73(5), 30–51. https://doi.org/10.1509/jmkg.73.5.30
Schroeder, J.E., & Borgerson, J.L. (2018). The death of brands: Why consumers are saying no to buying brands and what to do about it. *Journal of Brand Management*, 25(1), 6–18.
Sobande, F. (2019). Woke-washing: "intersectional" femvertising and branding "woke" bravery. *European Journal of Marketing*, 54(11), 2723–2745. https://doi.org/10.1108/ejm-02-2019-0134
Sobande, F. (2024). *Big brands are watching you: Marketing social justice and digital culture*. Oakland, CA: University of California Press.
Suchman, M.C. (1995). Managing legitimacy: Strategic and institutional approaches. *Academy of Management Review*, 20(3), 571. https://doi.org/10.2307/258788
Thompson, C.J., & Arsel, Z. (2004). The Starbucks brandscape and consumers' (anticorporate) experiences of globalization. *Journal of Consumer Research*, 31(3), 631–642.
Varadarajan, P.R., & Menon, A. (1988). Cause-related marketing: A coalignment of marketing strategy and corporate philanthropy. *Journal of Marketing*, 52(3), 58. https://doi.org/10.2307/1251450
Verlegh, P.W.J. (2024). Perspectives: A research-based guide for brand activism. *International Journal of Advertising*, 43(2), 388–402. https://doi.org/10.1080/02650487.2023.2228117
Vogel, D. (2007). *The market for virtue: The potential and limits of corporate social responsibility*. Washington, DC: Brookings Institution Press.
Vredenburg, J. (2020). Brand activism: What, when, where and how, translating theory into practice. *Journal of Brand Management*, 27(4), 289–303. https://doi.org/10.1057/s41262-020-00215-6
Vredenburg, J., Kapitan, S., Spry, A., & Kemper, J.A. (2020). Brands taking a stand: Authentic brand activism or woke washing? *Journal of Public Policy and Marketing*, 39(4), 444–460. https://doi.org/10.1177/0743915620947359
Wagner, T., Lutz, R.J., & Weitz, B.A. (2009). Corporate hypocrisy: Overcoming the threat of inconsistent corporate social responsibility perceptions. *Journal of Marketing*, 73(6), 77–91. https://doi.org/10.1509/jmkg.73.6.77
Zizek, S. (1997). *Plague of fantasies*. London: Verso Books.

5 The Ethical Responsibility of Visibility

This final chapter interrogates the dynamics of visibility and invisibility, shaped by selective empathy, that characterize brand responses to global crises. While Western societies largely condemn territorial annexation in Ukraine, atrocities in Gaza and Lebanon often encounter widespread indifference. Many brands reflect this selective disengagement, choosing silence over acknowledgment or involvement with these pressing issues. The ongoing wars in Gaza and Lebanon expose the limitations of brand activism (Khamis, 2023; Vredenburg et al., 2020; Moorman, 2020), particularly in its capacity to address global justice. This chapter critically examines whether brands bear ethical responsibilities beyond their market imperatives, questioning the extent to which they can—or should—act as agents of accountability and justice in an unequal and divided global society.

Throughout this book, I argue that when brands align with social causes, their involvement must be analyzed not as an extension of their promotional strategies but as a mode of engaging with ethical narratives that demand scrutiny. As demonstrated in Chapters 2 and 3, the alignment between brands and ethical values cannot merely claim coherence; it must also demonstrate an ethical infrastructure that extends beyond surface-level declarations. Chapter 4 further highlights how consumer expectations are not passive but actively interrogate the legitimacy of brands' moral claims, exposing gaps in their ethical stances.

As Hoppner and Vadakkepatt (2019) suggest, moral authority is a performative condition—a credibility established within specific discursive and material frameworks. This leads to the question of moral ontology. Moral ontology, in this context, does not merely describe the ethical commitments a brand claims but interrogates how those commitments emerge from relational practices grounded in justice and accountability. It examines the capacity of a brand's activism to be recognized as morally coherent within the interrelation of its stated values, material practices, and public engagements. The paradox of brand activism, as explored throughout this book, lies in its simultaneous reliance on and critique of transactional logics. While brand activism positions itself as a challenge to neoliberal norms, it often sustains the very mechanisms

DOI: 10.4324/9781003105893-5

it seeks to disrupt. This epistemological shift compels us to reconsider brand activism not simply as a communicative act but as a process of constituting ethical relations with tangible social and political implications.

The following section synthesizes the main arguments developed in the preceding chapters, situating them within a broader exploration of the limitations of brand activism as a framework for rethinking moral engagement in media and advertising practices. This will be followed by an explanation of the goals of this chapter and a detailed development of my reasoning.

In Chapter 2, I demonstrated how brands increasingly employ empathetic narratives to signal their alignment with social justice causes, aiming to connect with consumers on a deeper level. This strategy can effectively raise awareness and contribute to positive change by drawing attention to important issues and demonstrating corporate solidarity. Empathy, in this context, humanizes brands and fosters a sense of shared humanity, enhancing consumer loyalty and support through emotional connections that resonate with their values. The way in which they articulate stories of suffering, solidarity and moral responsibility influences how audiences perceive and engage with the vulnerable other.

Chapter 3 shifts focus to the role of digital platforms in shaping public engagement with brand activism, particularly through the lens of empathy-based narratives. The analysis reveals how these platforms, driven by algorithms that prioritize content based on similarity, often reinforce existing marginalizations by simplifying complex social causes. Such representations risk reducing the struggles of marginalized groups to narratives that serve the brand's image rather than advancing meaningful social change. The chapter evaluates how audiences interpret and respond to these empathetic portrayals, highlighting the ethical implications for advertisers. This investigation is essential for understanding the limitations and potential of empathetic messaging in influencing consumer behavior and addressing social injustice.

In Chapter 4, I addressed the growing pressure on brands to engage with social causes as consumers increasingly scrutinize their ethical stances, particularly through social media. Interviewees expressed heightened expectations for brands to tackle issues like human rights, environmental sustainability, and political conflicts. While brand activism can effectively raise awareness and generate empathy, it frequently leans on surface-level stories that, while compelling, divert attention from the complex, underlying forces that fuel these issues. This scrutiny has made brands more susceptible to consumer skepticism, especially when they fail to deliver on their promises of genuine, political engagement. Consumers are aware of performative gestures and are critical of brands that engage with "safe" causes, applauding those that demonstrate a deeper, more consistent political commitment. Moreover, consumers negotiate the idea that they should take moral responsibility for their spending choices, questioning the extent to which their purchases can influence larger corporate practices. However, there remains skepticism about consumers' ability to influence large corporations to make substantial changes, reflecting a recognition of the limitations and potential contradictions inherent in brand activism.

In the pages that follow, I revisit the tension between visibility and invisibility—a recurring ethical issue in brand activism introduced in Chapter 1—to analyze how brand narratives selectively amplify certain social causes while marginalizing others. This selective approach, evident in the silence surrounding issues like the Gaza conflict contrasted with vocal support for Western-centric causes, underscores a strategic manipulation of narratives that reinforces existing power structures. However, the rise of activism driven by younger consumers, exemplified by movements such as Boycott, Divestment, Sanctions (BDS) (Barghouti, 2021) and #Blockout2024 (Rucker, 2024), has intensified demands for brand accountability. Rather than fully rejecting consumerism, consumers are increasingly urging their favorite brands to take a clear stance on causes they deem important, effectively elevating brands to the status of moral authorities. These evolving expectations carry significant implications for the future of brand activism, indicating a potential shift in how brands address social justice and engage with their communities.

The Violence of Invisibility

The ethical challenge of brand activism lies in its selective visibility of social causes, where some are highlighted while others are strategically ignored. This strategic omission within the narrative of empathy, as explored in Chapters 1 and 2, reveals a paradox within activist brand campaigns. While these campaigns may bring certain social causes to the fore, utilizing media and advertising to raise awareness, this visibility is often selective and incomplete. It tends to mask the underlying systemic conditions that necessitate activism in the first place (Crane and Matten, 2016, p. 365). The emphasis on branding and marketability often leads to the simplification of social injustice into easily digestible narratives that fit neatly into marketing campaigns (Chouliaraki, 2012, p. 15). This creates a scenario where visibility serves as a form of obfuscation, obscuring deeper societal inequalities and the role corporations often play in sustaining them.

By prioritizing narratives and causes that resonate with Western audiences, often through a lens of pity or saviorism (Chouliaraki, 2012, p. 28), brand activism can recklessly reinforce a hierarchy that privileges certain lives and experiences over others. This perpetuates the "violence of invisibility" (Fraser, 1997, p. 25), rendering the struggles and perspectives of marginalized communities in the Global South invisible or less important (Said, 1995; Spivak, 1998). In Chapter 1, I observed that the Gaza war serves as a stark example of this selective empathy. Despite the severe humanitarian crisis and widespread devastation, there was a notable lack of support from global brands for Palestinians. To counter this, I draw on the theoretical contributions developed in previous chapters to advocates for a more inclusive approach to social justice that amplifies marginalized voices and challenges dominant Western perspectives. This normative approach calls for a shift toward genuine ethical engagement, holding corporations accountable, and fostering a more equitable global society through critical consumer activism and systemic change.

While brand activism has undoubtedly addressed issues of race and racial justice, as evident in campaigns like Nike's support for the Black Lives Matter movement (Chapter 2), the disparate attention to and engagement with conflicts impacting the Global South exposes inconsistencies and preferential activism within this practice. As Iqani (2016) notes, such disparities suggest a strategic alignment with causes that appeal to brands' primary consumer base, often located in Western markets, while neglecting issues that do not directly influence their brand image or profitability. The stark contrast between the relative silence of prominent brands and the advertising industry on the Gaza war and their vocal activism on conflicts predominantly affecting Western populations, like the Ukrainian war, raises concerns about a possible "logic of narrative control" (Said, 1995, p. 7) at play. This raises a profound ethical question: can activism that is contingent on market interests ever escape the logic of commodification, or does it inevitably transform genuine moral commitments into mere transactions, thereby undermining the very ideals it purports to uphold?

This selective engagement underscores the power dynamics at play, where the Global North dictates which suffering and whose victimhood are deemed worthy of attention and empathy. As Chouliaraki (2024) notes, "It is this dynamic of power that historically renders Western, white sufferers more visible than non-Western, nonwhite 'others' in Euro-American public spheres" (p. 43). The narratives brands choose to amplify are heavily influenced by systemic biases, such as white supremacy and Western-centric perspectives, that privilege certain lives and experiences over others (Mignolo, 2011, p. 45). This selectivity is not merely a reflection of geographical and political interests, but also a manifestation of deeper societal prejudices embedded in the fabric of global power structures (Mignolo, 2011, p. 68). The plight of those in the Global North, often portrayed as more relatable and deserving of sympathy, is foregrounded while the suffering of those in the Global South is relegated to the periphery of public consciousness (Morris, 2010, p. 12).

Jonathan Glazer's Oscar-winning film *Zone of Interest* (2023) serves as a chilling illustration of the insidious logic of violence through invisibility. By focusing on the seemingly mundane lives of Nazi officers living next to Auschwitz, the film reveals how the Höss family normalizes and compartmentalizes their participation in atrocities. This normalization is achieved through a deliberate erasure of the suffering taking place just beyond a wall. This invisibility is not merely a physical separation; it is a psychological and emotional barrier that allows the idyllic family to disassociate themselves from the consequences of their actions. This invisibility, both in the film and in contemporary brand activism, goes beyond mere physical erasure; it seeks to silence the oppressed, stripping them of their agency and voice. As Glazer (2024) himself highlighted in his poignant comparison of the ongoing conflict in Gaza to his film during his Oscar acceptance speech, the victims of systemic violence are often rendered invisible through normalization, their suffering obscured to maintain the comfort and complicity of those in power.

The extent of suffering of Gaza's victims, much like the hidden victims in the film, remains largely obscured from the Western world's consciousness. Physical and metaphorical barriers render their plight invisible, enabling those in power to continue their lives undisturbed. As Morse (2018) argues, media coverage of suffering often adheres to selective logics, granting visibility to deaths and tragedies deemed politically or culturally significant while obscuring others. This selective empathy, where some suffering is acknowledged while other suffering is ignored, epitomizes the violence of invisibility (Dotson, 2011). It fuels injustice by maintaining a comfortable distance between beneficiaries and victims of the system. This absence of awareness is not limited to geopolitical conflicts; it can also manifest in the realm of brand activism and promotional communication (West and McAllister, 2023).

As Edwards (2018) observes, the politics of visibility governs which narratives are rendered legible within public discourse, amplifying voices that sustain dominant systems of power while silencing those that challenge their authority. Building on this, Cronin's (2018) analysis of branding capitalism demonstrates how cultural intermediaries act as mediators of meaning, embedding exclusions within the representational logics of advertising and promotional culture. These exclusions are not arbitrary but are shaped by economic imperatives, as Bourne's (2020) exploration of market moralities reveals. Bourne argues that visibility is strategically constructed to align with market-driven ideologies, ensuring that public narratives serve economic logics while preserving existing power relations. Taken together, these perspectives expose visibility as more than a passive reflection of reality; it is an active process through which systemic power defines the parameters of perception and knowledge. In this way, the violence of invisibility persists, shaping both geopolitical crises and the commodified frameworks of brand activism.

The suffering of victims (Chouliaraki, 2024) like those in Gaza becomes an externality, conveniently disregarded as long as our lives remain undisturbed. As Fraser argues, selective empathy enables a form of 'misframing' (Fraser, 2013, p. 22), whereby the true scope and nature of systemic injustice are hidden from view. When individual narratives of suffering are elevated and the structural conditions that create such suffering go unaddressed, brand activism risks reinforcing existing power imbalances and perpetuating systemic inequalities. This partial engagement, which Fraser terms 'misrecognition' (Fraser, 1999, p. 21), "denies some individuals and groups the possibility of participating on a par with others in social interaction," and thus fails to challenge the root causes of oppression and instead fuels a cycle of marginalization and invisibility.

The violence of invisibility, which fundamentally challenges the idea that brand activism can genuinely raise awareness of social causes, prompts a critical question: can brand activism truly be a force for social change if it perpetuates the same dynamics of exclusion that it purports to combat? By selectively highlighting certain issues while ignoring others, brand activism often reproduces a moralistic vision of society, reducing complex social realities to simplified narratives that are easy to market. As Sobande (2024, p. 190) notes, "Institutions and individuals who are intent on becoming moral arbiters, or who already assume such a position, include commercial brands, social enterprise entities, and academic disciplines." In positioning themselves as moral arbiters, brands engage in selective visibility, where attention is contingent on how well a social cause aligns with corporate interests and marketing opportunities, rather than a genuine commitment to human rights. As a result, brand activism risks distorting public understanding of social justice, presenting an appearance of ethical engagement while continuing to benefit from the very systems of inequality it claims to challenge.

In the context of advertising, this selective focus often means prioritizing issues that resonate with Western audiences, thereby neglecting the diverse and interconnected struggles faced by communities worldwide. By reproducing these narrow narratives, brands not only reinforce existing power structures but also contribute to the erasure of marginalized voices. It is of utmost importance to move beyond this selective visibility to actively engage with and bring to light the hidden injustices that sustain global inequality and oppression (Juris and Pleyers, 2009, p. 73). Such an approach is necessary to engender a more comprehensive understanding of global struggles, which is essential for dismantling the structures on which systemic injustice depend. This understanding sets the stage for the following section, "The Everyday Complicity," which examines how consumers' uncritical acceptance of these sanitized narratives further entrenches systemic injustices, highlighting the need for a more critical and inclusive approach to social justice (vanHoose and Savini, 2017, p. 307).

While a more inclusive and comprehensive approach to social justice is undeniably necessary, we must consider whether expecting commercial brands to lead this charge is realistic or even appropriate. Brands are fundamentally driven by profit motives and may not always be equipped or incentivized to address the full spectrum of human experiences, particularly those that challenge prevailing power structures or disrupt their target markets (Cronin, 2018). This concern about the limitations of profit-driven entities in leading social justice initiatives is echoed in the work of McChesney (2000), who argues that commercial media, driven by profit motives, are often ill-equipped to challenge the status quo or promote radical social change. However, this does not absolve consumers from their responsibilities. As Silverstone (2002) explains, complicity and collusion can hinder our ability to critically assess social, civic and moral matters. Complicity involves accepting media portrayals without question, while collusion involves a form of self-deception, whereby we neglect our moral responsibility toward ambiguous expressions of empathy. It is important to engage actively with brand activism and question the narratives presented, rather than passively consuming them and further reinforcing the invisibility of those who are not deemed worthy of attention.

As Chouliaraki (2012, p. 156) argues, it is crucial for audiences to develop a sense of active responsibility and moral engagement. This ethical responsibility can also be extended to consumers, who must critically evaluate their role in supporting or challenging brand narratives. This means seeking out diverse perspectives and challenging the dominant narratives presented by brands and the media. Paradoxically, this form of critical engagement necessitates a reversal of traditional brand activism—transforming it into activism against brands when necessary, by holding them accountable for their social impact (Mukherjee and Banet-Weiser, 2012, p. 85). In recognizing the influence brands wield and insisting on transparency and accountability, consumers can shift from being passive recipients of commercial messaging to active agents of social change. In doing so, they help dismantle the cycle of invisibility and marginalization that brands often perpetuate, thereby contributing to a more just and equitable society.

A New Generation of Consumer Activists

In spring 2024, as I worked on this book, the protests against the Gaza war erupted across cities, campuses and social media, revealing a significant generational shift. Generation Z, once criticized as 'snowflakes' overly focused on safe spaces to engage with uncomfortable ideas or push themselves in challenging directions (Gopal, 2024), now demonstrates a profound and active resistance to injustice. These young people, including some of my students, refuse to accept passive indifference. They join protests, participate in rallies, boycott brands and utilize social media to amplify their voices and seek unfiltered, unbiased information beyond traditional media constraints. In rejecting the comforting certainty that things are as they should be and that brands inherently have the best intentions, they forge a path of conscientious activism and critical engagement with societal causes.

This global wave of youthful dissent, empowered by digital tools and a discerning eye (Bezbaruah and Trivedi, 2020), is reshaping the conversation around brand responsibilities and ethical practices. As Lekakis (2022, p. 184) observes, "If advertising sells 'wokeness', 'feminism', and 'sustainability', what is the role of consumers beyond subscribing to that ideology? Their role is to remain critical of simplified solutions to social change." This sentiment resonates with the actions of this new generation, who demand more than just performative activism from brands. They are increasingly aware of the power dynamics at play and refuse to be passive recipients of corporate messaging.

In the aftermath of the recent conflicts in Gaza and Lebanon, two significant elements have emerged that advertisers and marketers should consider carefully. First, the BDS movement was made popular among this generation of new consumer activists through social media and has ignited widespread calls for boycotts (Fenton, 2021; Chughtai et al., 2023; Vinall, 2024). Second, the Blockout 2024 movement, initiated by Generation Z on platforms like TikTok and Instagram, involves actively blocking brands, especially those that have not taken clear positions on contentious issues like Gaza (Complex, 2024; Dazed, 2024).

While these movements might appear to represent a dramatic shift in power dynamics, it is important to consider Lekakis' (2022, p. 43) caution:

> We need to understand that while the advent of digital/social/mobile media has both routinely and rebelliously reconfigured consumer activism, it is not a panacea. We can interrogate how consumer activist agency is constituted, mobilized, and connected to technologies, agencies, and meanings.

Thus, while these movements certainly exert pressure on brands and highlight a growing consumer desire for accountability, it remains to be seen whether they represent a truly novel phenomenon or a continuation of longstanding anti-consumerist and activist traditions, now amplified by digital platforms.

Their rejection of passive acceptance and demand for transparency and accountability are forcing brands to reconsider their positions and actions; some of those brands include Starbucks, McDonald's and Zara (Chapter 1). This emerging movement recognizes and actively denounces the trivial treatment of moral problems by brands, requiring more than mere performative gestures and seeking to hold corporations accountable for their tangible actions and stances on critical issues. The refusal to accept the violence of invisibility signals a growing awareness among consumers that genuine, impactful change requires a deeper level of engagement beyond consumerism. However, further research is needed to assess the long-term impact and effectiveness of these movements in driving meaningful change in brand behavior and corporate social responsibility.

A notable illustration of this phenomenon is the case of KFC in Algeria. The fast-food chain is one of many brands that have been impacted by boycott campaigns over their perceived support for the Israeli occupation (Zbeedat, 2024). In a January statement, the BDS movement listed KFC's sister company Pizza Hut (both owned by Yum Brands) as a complicit company to boycott (BDS, 2024). Although the ban was specifically targeted at Pizza Hut, its association with KFC under the same parent company was enough to spark a broader boycott against KFC as well. The opening of a KFC branch in Algeria in April 2024 triggered public outcry and large protests. Social media platforms amplified the outrage, with demonstrators demanding the closure of the new restaurant (Lucente, 2024).

The backlash was so significant that the store was compelled to reopen without its iconic branding, functioning as an anonymous fried chicken establishment under KFC management. This example lends credence to Naomi Klein's critique of corporate globalization and its potential for cultural appropriation and insensitivity (2009/2001). The impact of these boycotts extended beyond Algeria, as KFC Malaysia also temporarily closed outlets in May 2024 amid the Gaza boycott (Al Jazeera, 2024). These protests and their impact on global brands like KFC reflect a broader trend where local activism in the Global South is increasingly challenging and shaping global brand strategies (Brazzoduro, 2020; Sajed, 2023).

The effect of the boycotts is a dent in profits for these corporations on BDS's blacklist. At the time of writing, it has been concluded from the presentation of financial reports for several companies traded on the New York stock exchange, including Coca Cola, Starbucks and McDonald's, that these boycotts have led to a drop in sales in the Middle East and Southeast Asia (FT Reporters, 2024; Lee et al., 2024). Protests in the Global South often arise from historical grievances (Spivak, 1988) and ongoing socio-political struggles rooted in colonial histories (Said, 1995). Their dissidence at the local level, producing tangible effects in the global context, demonstrates the critical role of post-colonial perspectives in understanding contemporary consumer activism. These protests, when resonating globally, challenge traditional power structures and compel a re-examination of corporate practices and their alignment with ethical standards (Bhabha, 2019, originally published 1994; Iquani, 2016, p. 16). The impact of such movements extends beyond immediate localities, affecting global perceptions and prompting similar actions in the Global North (Fanon, 1983). Therefore, actions in the Global South can significantly influence corporate decisions on a global scale.

Movements like BDS and #Blockout2024, with significant participation from activists in the Global South, actively reject condescending approaches to social injustice. They challenge brands to transcend performative allyship and engage in meaningful, substantive actions aligned with principles of justice and equality. As Özturan and Grinstein (2022, p. 77) emphasize, the rise of a globally conscious consumer segment expects brands to act as agents of positive change, even taking stances on geopolitical conflicts like Ukraine and Gaza.

It is crucial to note that these movements are not inherently anti-capitalist or anti-consumerist. Rather, they recognize brands as legitimate political actors and demand that they engage in meaningful conversations about social injustice (Narayanan, 2022). This marks a departure from previous protest movements, which often focused on boycotting or disrupting corporate activities. The current wave of activism seeks to hold brands accountable and leverage their influence to promote social justice.

Though consumer pressure might appear to demand greater accountability from brands, this dynamic can also be understood as a strategic exercise of corporate influence. Brands do not merely respond to moral imperatives but actively influence consumer subjectivities—an ongoing process through which individuals' perceptions, emotional orientations, and ethical commitments are aligned with market logics. This process, often conceptualized as *emotional capitalism* (Chouliaraki, 2024; Illouz, 2007; Lazzarato, 2014), reveals how corporations frame moral engagement in ways that ultimately serve their profit-driven agendas. By constructing emotional narratives around ethical concerns, brands transform moral imperatives into opportunities for consumer engagement, reducing complex social and political issues into commodified moral spectacles.

This *production of subjectivity* not only co-opts moral engagement but also undermines the transformative potential of activism. Rather than empowering consumers to interrogate structural inequities, it perpetuates cycles where even urgent ethical concerns (Pöyry and Laaksonen, 2022, p. 22) are subsumed within the logic of consumerism. Brands, in their role as mediators of social and political discourse, strategically leverage morality to cultivate affective ties with audiences. This dynamic reflects what Micheletti and Stolle (2008) describe as a form of "political consumerism," in which the boundaries between ethical engagement and market participation blur. Yet, rather than disrupting these boundaries, such strategies reinforce the underlying capitalist frameworks (Harvey, 2005), sustaining systems of power that prioritize economic imperatives over meaningful social transformation.

This process of subjectivity production is further complicated by the fact that brand activism, while global in reach, manifests differently across various cultural, political and economic contexts. Brand activism might be a global phenomenon, but it does not manifest uniformly across different contexts; instead, it is a product of situated, interwoven power dynamics that vary significantly across countries. Local cultural, political and economic factors profoundly shape how brand activism takes form, underscoring the importance of understanding these specific contexts (Gürhan-Canli et al., 2018). This is crucial because historical and social contexts not only influence our perceptions but also shape our understanding of concepts like power, knowledge and subjectivity. Foucault's work is particularly relevant here (1977), as he explicates how norms are produced and sustained within these power structures, thereby challenging the presumed universality of ethical standards.

Foucault's analysis of power is central to his anti-normative approach, which posits that power is not merely repressive but also productive and pervasive, functioning through various institutions and discourses. His focus on the dynamics of power—rather than moral evaluations of power as inherently good or bad—encourages a better understanding of political relations that transcends simplistic normative judgments (Foucault, 1980). While Foucault's anti-normative stance provides crucial insights into the fluidity and complexity of power (Kelly, 2018), I argue that a normative position is indispensable in the context of brand activism for evaluating and guiding ethical actions.

The key distinction lies in the application of moral principles: whereas Foucault seeks to uncover how power operates without passing moral judgment, my normative approach insists on the necessity of ethical standards to assess the social impact of brand actions. This perspective is vital for holding brands accountable, ensuring that their actions align with broader moral principles, and advancing a more equitable society. In contrast to Foucault's analysis of power, my approach highlights the prescriptive role of ethics in guiding brand behavior toward justice and equity—an argument that I will expand upon in the following section.

The Ethical Responsibility of Visibility

The ethical responsibility of visibility, a concept I have developed at the intersection of ethics and social justice, demands a critical self-awareness from practitioners, particularly advertisers. It calls for intentional choices that contribute to equitable representation, rather than mirroring market trends. This responsibility, as I conceptualize it, encompasses the deliberate choice to reject certain narratives and perspectives, contributing to the construction of a 'visibility regime'—a system that privileges some voices while obscuring others. These choices are inherently ethical, as they directly impact the representation and recognition of diverse voices and experiences. The ethical responsibility of visibility, viewed through the lens of recognition philosophy, extends beyond measly acknowledgment toward the emphatic affirmation of dignity and humanity for all individuals and causes (Honneth, 1996; Taylor, 1992). This implies a moral imperative for equitable consideration, challenging the selective empathy that often characterizes brand activism.

Butler (2009) highlights a central ethical dilemma: how do we reconcile universal principles, like valuing all lives equally, with the stark realities of lived experiences marked by inequality? Selective empathy often intensifies this tension. Recognition theory reveals how power structures determine whose suffering is acknowledged and whose lives are deemed worthy of protection. This challenges the practicality of universal ethical principles. In essence, there's a disconnect between the ideal of treating everyone ethically and the reality where marginalized groups are often overlooked. This selective visibility, as Spivak (1988) notes, results in certain narratives dominating public discourse while others are silenced.

This dynamic is further explored by Fraser (2005, 2023), who posits that social justice requires both the redistribution of resources and the recognition of cultural and social identities. However, the causes that garner attention and empathy are often those that align with prevailing power structures, and thereby become visible, while those deemed less marketable or too challenging to these structures are relegated to the shadows of invisibility. This intimates how visibility and recognition are often dictated by marketability and alignment with dominant societal norms, rather than by the inherent merit or urgency of the cause itself.

The challenge of applying normative theory to brand activism lies in translating its abstract concepts and principles into concrete actions for practitioners. This requires not only a deep understanding of ethical theories but also an appreciation of the social, political and economic realities that shape individual and collective behavior. This echoes Foucault's (1980) concept of the genealogy of power, which highlights how power relations are embedded in and shape social practices and discourses. The successful application of normative theory to brand activism necessitates a praxis-oriented approach, wherein practitioners actively engage with and analyze the power structures that shape consumer culture (Smith, 2008). As Habermas (1990) maintains, ethical norms are not static but must be continuously re-examined and adapted through rational discourse and communicative processes. This ongoing reflection is essential in a globalized society, particularly in dynamic industries like marketing and advertising, where the application of normative theory demands constant adjustment to remain relevant and effective in addressing evolving ethical challenges.

Crucially, practitioners need to recognize the profound link between applied ethics and epistemic failure. The condition of invisibility, a direct consequence of unexamined biases and power structures within these industries, not only denies recognition to marginalized groups but also constitutes an epistemic failure (Fricker, 2007, p. 7) and, more insidiously, a form of epistemic violence (Spivak, 1988). By choosing which causes to empathize with, marketers and advertisers shape not only moral priorities but also the very framework of knowledge itself, deciding what is known, acknowledged and understood in society (Fricker, 2007, p. 2). This exclusion of certain realities from the collective perspective constitutes a deeper failure in the processes that determine what is recognized and valued as knowledge (King, 2017, p. 259).

This epistemic failure is further compounded by a lack of critical self-awareness within the marketing and advertising professions, neglecting the ethical duty to accurately represent others. As Medina argues, the epistemic failure is also "a failure in self-knowledge and a failure in the knowledge of others… because the lack of familiarity and critical awareness of one's social positionality involves not knowing oneself in relation to one's relevant others" (2013, p. 37). Therefore, the invisibility of marginalized perspectives becomes a double epistemic failure—a failure to acknowledge certain experiences and a failure to recognize one's own role in perpetuating this invisibility.

The recognition of this connection between epistemic failure and the responsibility of visibility is crucial for ethical brand activism. Marketers and advertisers, by failing to critically assess their own positionality and the power relationships in which they partake, inadvertently uphold a skewed epistemic framework that privileges certain narratives while erasing others. This is not just a passive omission but an active construction of what is considered legitimate knowledge in the public sphere. Consequentially, dominant perspectives are continually reinforced and those of the marginalized are systematically silenced. In this cycle of injustice, the marginalized are denied the opportunity to participate in shaping the narratives that define their reality.

Although not explicitly political actors, advertisers and marketers exert considerable influence in shaping public discourse and cultural norms, particularly when engaging in brand activism or cause-related marketing. The ethical responsibility of ensuring equitable representation aligns with the broader goal of communicating "to communicate brands' moral competency, defined in terms of moral sensitivity, moral vision, and moral integration" and demonstrate "moral exemplarity by pioneering moral precepts, supporting emerging moral leaders whose values align with theirs, or even creating their own social movement" (Sibai et al., 2021, p. 1663). This imperative is further vindicated by growing consumer and activist demands for accountability (Skotnicki, 2018; Brochado et al., 2017) as owell as an evolving understanding of corporate social responsibility (CSR) that prioritizes social justice and equity alongside environmental and social well-being (Fordham & Robinson, 2019; Ashrafi et al., 2020).

This commitment to social responsibility necessitates a deeper engagement with the ethical principles underpinning industry actions, ensuring strategies are not only effective but also morally sound. This alignment fosters ethical integrity and establishes a foundation for practices that resonate with both consumers and society. The following three arguments, presented as ethical challenges, encapsulate the key concerns about brand activism raised in this book. These arguments do not condemn the industry as inherently unethical but rather stem from an empirically informed ethical analysis—grounded in research and interviews (Chapters 3 and 4)—regarding the practical application of moral theories in branded activist campaigns. This disconnect between theory and practice is not merely theoretical; it directly impacts consumer perception and trust in brands.

Regrettably, based on my professional experience as a practitioner and researcher, applied ethics have often devolved into compliance-driven exercises, where moral reasoning is reduced to a checklist rather than being an integral part of decision-making. Normative theory, however, offers a crucial counterpoint, providing the philosophical foundation necessary to address these deontological shortcomings by demanding a deeper examination of the moral implications of marketing practices. It challenges practitioners to engage critically with the ethical underpinnings of their actions, ensuring that their strategies actively combat epistemic injustice. To understand these ethical problems, I have synthesized the key arguments presented in this book:

The **first argument** highlights how empathy, as it is utilized in brand activism, frequently relies on moralizing narratives that obscure the deeper, systemic roots of social injustice (Hopkins, 2017, p. 128). This framing is problematic because it tends to simplify and sentimentalize complex social realities, thereby hindering critical engagement with the structural causes of injustice. By capitalizing on social justice movements through feel-good narratives and overly positive portrayals of their initiatives (Zyglidopoulos et al., 2019), brands risk creating a veneer of progress that can overshadow genuine efforts to address underlying social problems (Crane and Matten, 2016).

Sobande (2024, p. 193) argues that the notion of any brand presenting a unified moral, social, or political stance is "fundamentally fragile," as a brand's image is carefully constructed and represents the work of many individuals with differing perspectives. This raises ethical concerns about the instrumentalization of empathy: is it being used to genuinely engage with and address social injustice, or is it primarily a means for moralizing society (Ahmed, 2014; Hopkins, 2017; Boltanski and Thevenot, 2006) that glosses over the need for systemic change? The challenge here is ensuring that empathy is not reduced to a vehicle of a "self-oriented morality, where doing good to others is about 'how I feel'" (Chouliaraki, 2013, p. 3), but is instead leveraged to cultivate a more critical and informed approach to social justice—one that emphasizes reasoned arguments and actionable solutions alongside emotional engagement. This tension between the instrumental and intrinsic value of empathy creates a dilemma: should an ethical responsibility of visibility demand that brands move beyond using empathy as a marketing tool altogether? The answer to this question is a complex one, as empathy and emotions are defining tools of storytelling.

While consumer activists are calling for brands to take a stand, the ethical responsibility of visibility necessitates an approach that prioritizes accountability, avoids misrepresentation, and respects the complexities of these causes. Let's consider a hypothetical scenario: Nike decides to produce a commercial featuring Colin Kaepernick in a Gaza refugee camp, expressing solidarity with Palestinians. They also release a new Air Max sneaker adorned with the Palestinian flag colors, advocating for Palestinian independence. Such a campaign would undoubtedly spark controversy. Critics, including myself, would likely accuse Nike of capitalizing on the suffering of 'distant others' and commodifying a complex political struggle. While the campaign might be perceived as cynical and exploitative, it also highlights a genuine ethical dilemma.

It is clear why such a campaign could easily cross the lines of both misappropriation and misrepresentation. The ethical dilemma arises specifically from the tension between the potential positive impact of the campaign—such as raising awareness and mobilizing support for a marginalized cause—and the potential harm of reducing a longstanding political struggle to the level of a consumer product and a marketing strategy. The risk is that Nike's actions, however well-intentioned, may be perceived as performative activism, where the emphasis is more on bolstering the brand's image than on genuinely advocating for meaningful change. This approach not only risks trivializing the cause but also raises serious concerns about cultural appropriation and the possibility that a multinational corporation could profit from a conflict without fully understanding its complexities or contributing to sustainable solutions.

Brand activism falters when it extends storytelling beyond the authentic experiences of impacted communities or reduces complex social problems to simplistic symbols. Critics may argue that expecting marketers to authentically engage with these issues is unrealistic, given their focus on profit, but the role they play in shaping cultural narratives demands ethical accountability. Advertising may not be a political force, but its influence on public discourse means that brands choosing to engage in activism must handle these issues with care. Rather than simply dismissing concerns, I argue that when brands venture into activism, marketers and advertisers should do so responsibly, ensuring their storytelling does not trivialize or distort the causes they decide to support. While marketers are not expected to lead systemic change, they should avoid misrepresenting or diluting the struggles they seek to address, recognizing their impact on public conversations.

Paradoxically, this critique of unrealistic expectation from the industry seemingly contradicts the demands of consumer activists who boycott brands for not taking a stance on issues like the war in Gaza. Therefore, marketers must critically examine not only the messages they convey but also the broader implications of rendering certain issues visible, particularly the risk of misrepresentation or misappropriation. The imperative is to ensure that visibility serves not just corporate interests, but genuinely enhances public awareness and understanding of complex issues. This necessitates a balanced approach that respects the dignity and intricacy of the causes, and refrains from oversimplification and exploitation.

My **second argument** is that empathy, especially when exercised from a position of privilege, often fails to create meaningful change for those it aims to support.

When individuals try to empathize by imagining themselves in another's situation, this effort often falls short—especially when the empathizer holds greater societal privilege or power (Decety and Cowell, 2015, p. 3). If brand activism provides inspiration, it typically benefits the privileged empathizer more than those they empathize with. This kind of empathetic exercise fails to fully comprehend the actual experiences of the other person, thereby entrenching the very hierarchies it seeks to dismantle (Segal, 2011, p. 270).

Moreover, if these corporate attempts to understand the Other are hindered by unrecognized privileges, the empathy they offer may come across as patronizing. Such skewed empathy usually results in apparent recognition rather than leading to genuine dialogue and understanding, and ultimately undermines efforts to achieve true solidarity (Pedwell, 2012, p. 287). Thus, brand activism requires critical ethical reflection on the use of empathy and the positionality of the empathizer, ensuring it engenders negotiation and genuine engagement rather than self-congratulation.

Some key questions must be addressed: Who has the right to champion a cause? Whose voices are authorized to speak on it? Is the brand's representation sufficient, accurate and appropriate? These ethical questions of ownership intersect with cultural conventions for representing social justice. Ethical reflection must begin by recognizing the privileged position of those with firsthand experience—they possess knowledge that grants them a legitimate stake in how their struggles are represented. This normative stance prevents the unchallenged transfer of ownership over social causes to brands, ensuring they cannot interpret and represent these issues without accountability.

My argument might be rooted in an unrealistic expectation of advertising's role in society. The inherent irony of brand activism lies in its attempt to foster equality while operating within a capitalist system that often perpetuates and profits from those same inequalities. Brands like Patagonia and Ben & Jerry's, despite their progressive stances and genuine efforts toward social and environmental responsibility, ultimately exist to generate profit. Their activism, while well-intentioned, can be seen as a form of emotional capitalism (Chouliaraki, 2024; Illouz, 2007; Lazzarato, 2014), where emotions and social causes are leveraged to create value and drive consumption. This tension between profit and activism brings us to a crucial question: if brands are willing to position themselves as moral actors in public disourse, should they not be held to the ethical standards of that role?

While advertising is not traditionally seen as a political actor, the practice of brand activism necessitates a critical ethical evaluation of its impact and unintended consequences. Critics may argue that expecting advertisers to drive social change imposes unrealistic demands, given their primary role in promotional communication. However, my argument is that once advertisers engage in activism and position themselves within social discourse, they take on specific responsibilities toward ensuring their messaging aligns with the ethical implications of the causes they champion. While advertising may not lead systemic change, its cultural and moral influence in shaping public narratives makes it necessary to hold advertisers accountable for how they represent social injustice.

A further objection might be that it is unreasonable to judge advertisers by standards that expect them to function as agents of social change. However, when advertisers intentionally engage in this type of storytelling, they blur the lines between commercial and political action, and with this shift comes an obligation to approach these issues thoughtfully. The ethical responsibility I propose does not ask advertisers to lead social movements but to ensure that their messaging does not distort or trivialize complex social and political struggles. By holding them to higher standards, we acknowledge their significant role in public discourse and encourage a more responsible form of brand activism that respects the integrity of the causes they claim to support.

My **third and final argument** is that marketers often prioritize causes that are marketable and widely appealing, rather than those that are most ethically urgent. This selectivity results in a distorted perception of morality, where ethical action is spurred on by popularity rather than a genuine commitment to social good. By focusing on 'safe' causes that are likely to resonate with their (Western) consumer base, corporations contribute to an understanding of what it means to be ethical, overshadowing the more challenging and critical issues that require attention.

This selective approach to moral engagement involves a strategic decision that balances market benefits against the potential risks of alienating certain customer groups (Mukherjee and Althuizen, 2020; Romani et al., 2015). Although this tactic may be practical from a business perspective (Lee and Kotler, 2023), it raises substantial ethical issues. According to Kantian ethics, moral actions must be guided by universal principles that apply regardless of the potential benefits or harms. The selective engagement of brand activism fails this test by treating morality as commodities to be exploited rather than as duties to be fulfilled. It reduces the moral imperative to address injustice to a strategic choice, thereby violating the principle of treating humanity—not just in others, but also in corporate actions (Drumwright and Murphy, 2004, 2009)—as an end in itself, rather than a means to an end. Consequently, only the most 'marketable' social causes receive attention and support, while less popular or more contentious issues are overlooked. This imbalance leads to a distorted perception of moral responsibility, where ethical considerations are driven more by public appeal than by the inherent merit of the causes.

Marketers need not make a simplistic binary choice but should develop the capacity to address the relationship between ethical responsibility and strategic imperatives. Both visibility and invisibility carry significant ethical weight, with the power to empower or marginalize social realities. The task at hand is to engage with these complexities thoughtfully, ensuring that actions promote genuine ethical engagement rather than merely enhance brand visibility. This necessitates a critical evaluation of which narratives are amplified and why, alongside a consideration of the broader societal impacts of selective visibility. In essence, the challenge is to embrace a form of activism that is deeply reflective, cognizant of its own power dynamics, and dedicated to advancing social causes with both authenticity and integrity.

Conclusion

Rather than offering prescriptive solutions, my work examines the limitations of relying exclusively on emotional empathy in brand activism. While I recognize the rhetorical power of storytelling, I argue that advertisers must confront the ethical responsibilities involved in constructing activist narratives. By integrating reasoned arguments with empathetic appeals, I advocate for an approach that encourages critical engagement with the ways these narratives contribute to public discourse on social justice. This requires an ongoing process of self-assessment, where brands interrogate their motivations and evaluate the broader consequences of their actions for audiences and the causes they claim to support. Therefore, I contend that resolving this tension requires a dynamic and sustained ethical commitment, ensuring that empathy serves as a catalyst for justice rather than a tool for exploitation or profit.

In closing, it is my hope that this book serves as a foundation for future scholarly inquiry, promoting critical dialogue and the development of ethically sound theoretical and practical applications within the field. Practitioners and scholars must continue to critically evaluate the impact and potential of brand activism in driving tangible social change, while remaining mindful of its limitations and inherent contradictions. Achieving this balance is no easy task. Practitioners must approach justice with sensitivity, avoiding the pitfalls of over-moralizing or instrumentalizing empathy. They must acknowledge the inherent paradoxes of brand activism without abandoning the pursuit of meaningful representation. Likewise, consumers and audiences must walk the fine line between offering altruism and maintaining a healthy skepticism about any rationale for benevolence that extends beyond self-interest. This balancing act reminds us that while advertising's primary objective is not to create a better society, it can at least prevent us from complacently assuming that we have already achieved it.

References

Ahmed, S. (2014). *The cultural politics of emotion* (2nd ed.). Edinburgh: Edinburgh University Press.

Al Jazeera. (2024, May 3). KFC Malaysia temporarily closes outlets amid Gaza boycott. *Al Jazeera*. https://www.aljazeera.com/economy/2024/5/3/kfc-malaysia-temporarily-closes-outlets-amid-gaza-boycott

Ashrafi, M., Magnan, G.M., Adams, M., & Walker, T.R. (2020). Understanding the conceptual evolutionary path and theoretical underpinnings of corporate social responsibility and corporate sustainability. *Sustainability*, 12(3), 760. https://doi.org/10.3390/su12030760

Barghouti, O. (2021). BDS: Nonviolent, globalized palestinian resistance to Israel's settler colonialism and apartheid. *Journal of Palestine Studies*, 50, 108–125.

Berestova, A., Kim, D.-Y., & Kim, S.-Y. (2022). Consumers' active reaction to brands taking stands on public issues on Twitter. *Sustainability*, 14(1), 567. https://doi.org/10.3390/su14010567

Bezbaruah, S., & Trivedi, J. (2020). Branded content: A bridge building Gen Z's consumer–brand relationship. *Vision The Journal of Business Perspective*, 24(3), 300–309. https://doi.org/10.1177/0972262920930167

Bhabha, H. K. (2019). *The location of culture*. 2nd ed. Abingdon, UK: Routledge. (Original work published 1994.)

Boltanski, L., & Thevenot, L. (2006). *On justification: Economies of worth* (C. Porter, Trans.). Princeton, NJ: Princeton University Press.

Bourne, C. (2020). *Trust, power and public relations in financial markets*. London: Routledge.

Boycott, Divestment, Sanctions (BDS) (2024). *Act now against these companies profiting from genocide*. Retrieved November 14, 2024, from https://www.bdsmovement.net/act-now-against-these-companies-profiting-from-genocide

Brazzoduro, A. (2020). Algeria, antifascism, and third worldism: An anticolonial genealogy of the western European new left (Algeria, France, Italy, 1957–1975). *The Journal of Imperial and Commonwealth History*, 48(5), 958–978. https://doi.org/10.1080/03086534.2020.1817232

Brochado, A., Teiga, N., & Oliveira-Brochado, F. (2017). The ecological conscious consumer behaviour: are the activists different? *International Journal of Consumer Studies*, 41(2), 138–146. https://doi.org/10.1111/ijcs.12321

Butler, J. (2009). *Frames of war: When is life grievable?* London: Verso.

Chouliaraki, L. (2012). The theatricality of humanitarianism: A critique of celebrity advocacy. *Communication and Critical/Cultural Studies*, 9(1), 1–21. https://doi.org/10.1080/14791420.2011.637055

Chouliaraki, L. (2013). *The ironic spectator: Solidarity in the age of post-humanitarianism* (1st ed.). Cambridge: Polity Press.

Chouliaraki, L. (2024). *Wronged: The weaponization of victimhood*. New York: Columbia University Press.

Chughtai, A., Ali, M., & Nolan, D. (2023, December 15). Boycotts and protests – how are people around the world defying Israel? *Al Jazeera*. https://www.aljazeera.com/news/2023/12/15/boycotts-and-protests-how-are-people-around-the-world-defying-israel

Complex. (2024, May 11). BlockOut 2024: *Social media users stage "digital guillotine" to protest celebrities who remain silent about Palestine*. Complex. https://www.complex.com/pop-culture/a/complexstaff3/blockout-2024-met-gala-protest

Couldry, N. (2010). *Why voice matters: Culture and politics after neoliberalism*. London: SAGE Publications.

Crane, A., & Matten, D. (2016). *Business ethics: Managing corporate citizenship and sustainability in the age of globalization* (4th ed.). Oxford: Oxford University Press.

Cronin, A.M. (2018). *Public relations capitalism: Promotional culture, publics and commercial Democracy*. London: Palgrave Macmillan.

Dazed. (2024, May 22). Blockout 2024: What should we realistically expect from celebrity activism? *Dazed*. https://www.dazeddigital.com/life-culture/article/62676/1/blockout-2024-what-should-we-actually-expect-from-celebrity-activism

Decety, J., & Cowell, J.M. (2015). Empathy, justice, and moral behavior. *AJOB Neuroscience*, 6(3), 3–14. https://doi.org/10.1080/21507740.2015.1047055

Dotson, K. (2011). Tracking epistemic violence, tracking practices of silencing. *Hypatia*, 26(2), 236–257. https://doi.org/10.1111/j.1527-2001.2011.01177.x

Drumwright, M.E., & Murphy, P.E. (2004). How advertising practitioners view ethics: Moral muteness, moral myopia, and moral imagination. *Journal of Advertising*, 33(2), 7–24. https://doi.org/10.1080/00913367.2004.10639158

Drumwright, M.E., & Murphy, P.E. (2009). The current state of advertising ethics: Industry and academic perspectives. *Journal of Advertising*, 38(1), 83–108. https://doi.org/10.2753/joa0091-3367380106

Edwards, L. (2018). *Understanding public relations: Theory, culture and society*. London: SAGE Publications.

Elliott, V. (2024, February 12). Satellite images point to indiscriminate Israeli attacks on Gaza's health care facilities. *Wired*. https://www.wired.com/story/israel-hamas-war-health-care-facilities-attack-study/

Fanon, F. (1983). *The wretched of the earth*. London: Penguin Books.

Fenton, N. (2021). Generation Z and brand activism. *Journal of Brand Strategy*, 10(3), 252–263.

Fordham, A.E., & Robinson, G.M. (2019). Identifying the social values driving corporate social responsibility. *Sustainability Science*, 14(5), 1409–1424. https://doi.org/10.1007/s11625-019-00720-w

Foucault, M. (1977). *Discipline and punish: The birth of the prison*. New York: Vintage Books.

Foucault, M. (1980). *Power/knowledge: Selected interviews and other writings, 1972–1977*. New York: Pantheon Books.

Fraser, N. (1997). *Justice interruptus: Critical reflections on the "postsocialist" condition*. Routledge.

Fraser, N. (1999). Social justice in the age of identity politics: Redistribution, recognition, and participation. In *Culture and economy after the cultural turn* (pp. 25–52). London: SAGE Publications Ltd.

Fraser, N. (2005). Reframing justice in a globalizing world. *New Left Review*, II(36), 69–88. https://newleftreview.org/issues/ii36/articles/nancy-fraser-reframing-justice-in-a-globalizing-world

Fraser, N. (2013). *Scales of justice: Reimagining political space in a globalizing world* (1st ed.). Cambridge: Polity Press.

Fraser, N. (2022). *Cannibal capitalism: How our system is devouring democracy, care, and the planet - and what we can do about it*. London and New York: Verso Books.
Fricker, M. (2007). *Epistemic injustice: Power and the ethics of knowing*. Oxford: Oxford University Press.
FT Reporters. (2024, August 5). Widespread boycotts in Muslim countries hammer western brands. *Financial Times*. https://www.ft.com/content/a2ee3452-ed34-45a1-8515-a88841c9ed31
Glazer, J. (2023). *The zone of interest*. https://www.imdb.com/title/tt7160372/
Glazer, J. (2024, March 11). Jonathan Glazer calls for end to "dehumanising" of victims in Gaza and Israel – video. *The Guardian*. https://www.theguardian.com/film/video/2024/mar/11/jonathan-glazer-oscars-speech-gaza-israel-video
Gopal, P. (2024). *In standing up for Gaza, US students have exposed the limits of free speech*. Prospectmagazine.co.uk. https://www.prospectmagazine.co.uk/politics/free-speech/65927/us-campus-protests-free-speech-gaza
Grassi, A. (2022). "We Like That It Matters!": Towards a Socially Sustainable Retail Store Brand Experience. *Sustainability*, 14(23), 16310. https://doi.org/10.3390/su142316310
Gürhan-Canli, Z., Sarial-Abi, G., & Hayran, C. (2018). Consumers and brands across the globe: Research synthesis and new directions. *Journal of International Marketing*, 26(1), 96–117. https://doi.org/10.1509/jim.17.0063
Habermas, J. (1990). *Moral consciousness and communicative action* (C. Lennardt & S.W. Nicholsen, Trans.). Cambridge, MA: MIT Press.
Harvey, D. (2005). *A brief history of neoliberalism*. Oxford: Oxford University Press.
Honneth, A. (1996). *The struggle for recognition: The moral grammar of social conflicts*. Cambridge: Polity Press.
Hopkins, P. (2017). *Mass moralizing: Marketing and moral storytelling*. Lexington, KY: Lexington Books.
Hoppner, J.J., & Vadakkepatt, G.G. (2019). Examining moral authority in the marketplace: A conceptualization and framework. *Journal of Business Research*, 95, 417–427. https://doi.org/10.1016/j.jbusres.2018.07.045
Illouz, E. (2007). *Cold intimacies: The making of emotional capitalism*. Cambridge: Polity Press.
Inocencio, R. (2024, October 25). *Israel accused of killing journalists in Lebanon strike and children as troops storm Gaza hospital*. CBS News. https://www.cbsnews.com/news/israel-war-iran-hamas-gaza-hezbollah-journalists-killed-lebanon-kamal-adwan-hospital/
Iqani, M. (2016). *Consumption, media and the Global South: Aspiration contested*. London: Palgrave Macmillan.
Juris, J.S., & Pleyers, G.H. (2009). Alter-activism: emerging cultures of participation among young global justice activists. *Journal of Youth Studies*, 12(1), 57–75. https://doi.org/10.1080/13676260802345765
Kayum Ahmed, A. (2023, November 16). *Israeli authorities' cutting of water leading to public health crisis in Gaza*. Human Rights Watch. https://www.hrw.org/news/2023/11/16/israeli-authorities-cutting-water-leading-public-health-crisis-gaza
Kelly, M.G.E. (2018). *For Foucault: Against normative political theory*. Albany, NY: State University of New York Press.
Khamis, S. (2023). *Branding diversity: New advertising and cultural strategies*. New York: Routledge.
King, M. (Ed.). (2017). *Tracing the epistemic condition*. Oxford University Press.
Klein, N. (2009). *No LOGO*. London: Picador.
Krever, M., & Nasser, I. (2024, November 14). Human Rights Watch accuses Israel of mass displacement in Gaza amounting to a war crime. *CNN*. https://www.cnn.

com/2024/11/14/middleeast/hrw-israel-gaza-displacement-war-crime-intl-hnk/index.html

Lazzarato, M. (2014). Signs and machines: Capitalism and the production of subjectivity (J.D. Jordan, Trans.). Los Angeles: Semiotext (E).

Lee, J.T., Tamo, O., & Meley, C. (2024, May 24). Anti-Israel boycotts hurting McDonald's, KFC in Asia, Mideast. Bloomberg.com. https://www.bloomberg.com/news/articles/2024-05-24/anti-israel-boycotts-hurting-mcdonald-s-kfc-in-asia-mideast?utm_source=website&utm_medium=share&utm_campaign=copy

Lee, N.R., & Kotler, P. (2023). *Social marketing: Behavior change for social good* (6th ed.). Los Angeles, CA: SAGE Publications.

Lekakis, E.J. (2022). *Consumer activism: Promotional culture and resistance*. London: SAGE Publications.

Lucente, A. (2024, April 17). Did Gaza protests force Algeria's first KFC restaurant to close? Al-Monitor: The Middle East's Leading Independent News Source since 2012. https://www.al-monitor.com/originals/2024/04/did-gaza-protests-force-algerias-first-kfc-restaurant-close

McChesney, R. W. (2000). *Rich media, poor democracy: Communication politics in dubious times*. University of Illinois Press.

Medina, J. (2013). Active ignorance, epistemic others, and epistemic friction. In *The epistemology of resistance* (pp. 27–55). Oxford: Oxford University Press.

Micheletti, M., & Stolle, D. (2008). Fashioning social justice through political consumerism, capitalism, and the internet1. *Cultural Studies*, 22(5), 749–769. https://doi.org/10.1080/09502380802246009

Mignolo, W.D. (2011). *The darker side of western modernity: Global futures, decolonial options*. Durham, NC: Duke University Press.

Moorman, C. (2020). Commentary: Brand activism in a political world. *Journal of Public Policy & Marketing*, 39(4), 388–392. https://doi.org/10.1177/0743915620945260

Morris, R. (Ed.). (2010). *Can the subaltern speak?: Reflections on the history of an idea*. New York: Columbia University Press.

Morse, T. (2018). *The Mourning News: Reporting Violent Death in a Global Age*. New York, NY: Peter Lang.

Mukherjee, S., & Althuizen, N. (2020). Brand activism: Does courting controversy help or hurt a brand? *International Journal of Research in Marketing*, 37(4), 772–788. https://doi.org/10.1016/j.ijresmar.2020.02.008

Mukherjee, R., & Banet-Weiser, S. (Eds.). (2012). *Commodity activism: Cultural resistance in neoliberal times*. New York: New York University Press. https://doi.org/10.18574/nyu/9780814763018.001.0001

Narayanan, S. (2022). Does Generation Z value and reward corporate social responsibility practices? *Journal of Marketing Management*, 38(9–10), 903–937. https://doi.org/10.1080/0267257x.2022.2070654

Özturan, P., & Grinstein, A. (2022). Impact of global brand chief marketing officers' corporate social responsibility and sociopolitical activism communication on Twitter. *Journal of International Marketing*, 30(3), 72–82. https://doi.org/10.1177/1069031x221104077

Pedwell, C. (2012). Economies of empathy: Obama, neoliberalism, and social justice. *Environment and Planning. D, Society & Space*, 30(2), 280–297. https://doi.org/10.1068/d22710

Pöyry, E., & Laaksonen, S.-M. (2022). Opposing brand activism: triggers and strategies of consumers' antibrand actions. *European Journal of Marketing*, 56(13), 261–284. https://doi.org/10.1108/ejm-12-2020-0901

Romani, S., Grappi, S., Zarantonello, L., & Bagozzi, R.P. (2015). The revenge of the consumer! How brand moral violations lead to consumer anti-brand activism. *Journal of Brand Management*, 22(8), 658–672. https://doi.org/10.1057/bm.2015.38

Rucker, S. (2024, May 15). What is Blockout 2024? List of celebrities people are blocking over Gaza stance. *iNews*. https://inews.co.uk/news/blockout-2024-celebrities-list-3057774?srsltid=AfmBOool_0QP3uY4Wifd9vUyFoke8HdmQflry53BfsSB95UXtlJZoBEE

Said, E.W. (1995). *Orientalism: Western conceptions of the orient*. New York: Penguin Books.

Sajed, A. (2023). Between Algeria and the world: anticolonial connectivity, aporias of national liberation and postcolonial blues. *Postcolonial Studies*, 26(1), 13–31. https://doi.org/10.1080/13688790.2023.2127655

Segal, E.A. (2011). Social empathy: A model built on empathy, contextual understanding, and social responsibility that promotes social justice. *Journal of Social Service Research*, 37(3), 266–277. https://doi.org/10.1080/01488376.2011.564040

Sibai, O., Mimoun, L., & Boukis, A. (2021). Authenticating brand activism: Negotiating the boundaries of free speech to make a change. *Psychology & Marketing*, 38(10), 1651–1669. https://doi.org/10.1002/mar.21477

Silverstone, R. (2002). Complicity and collusion in the mediation of everyday life. *New Literary History*, 33(4), 761–780. https://doi.org/10.1353/nlh.2002.0045

Skotnicki, T. (2018). Protest politics in the marketplace: Consumer activism in the corporate age. *Social Forces; a Scientific Medium of Social Study and Interpretation*, 97(1), e6. https://doi.org/10.1093/sf/soy054

Smith, J.D. (2008). *Normative theory and business ethics*. Lanham, MD: Rowman & Littlefield.

Sobande, F. (2024). *Big brands are watching you: Marketing social justice and digital culture*. Oakland, CA: University of California Press.

Spivak, G. (1988). Can the subaltern speak? In C. Nelson & L. Grossberg (Eds.), *Marxism and the interpretation of culture*. Urbana, IL: University of Illinois Press.

Taylor, C. (1992). *Multiculturalism and the politics of recognition: An essay by Charles Taylor* (A. Gutmann, Ed.). Princeton, NJ: Princeton University Press.

VanHoose, K., & Savini, F. (2017). The social capital of urban activism: Practices in London and Amsterdam. *City*, 21(3–4), 293–311. https://doi.org/10.1080/13604813.2017.1325207

Vinall, F. (2024, January 23). What's BDS, the movement to boycott Israel with a new social media following? Washington Post (Washington, DC: 1974). https://www.washingtonpost.com/world/2024/01/23/bds-movement-israel-boycott-brands/

Vredenburg, J., Kapitan, S., Spry, A., & Kemper, J.A. (2020). Brands taking a stand: Authentic brand activism or woke washing? *Journal of Public Policy & Marketing*, 39(4), 444–460. https://doi.org/10.1177/0743915620947359

West, E., & McAllister, M.P. (Eds.). (2023). *The Routledge companion to advertising and promotional culture* (2nd ed.). Abingdon, UK: Routledge.

Zbeedat, N. (2024, April 24). Algeria's first KFC restaurant closes amid Gaza protests, reopens without logo. *Haaretz*. https://www.haaretz.com/middle-east-news/2024-04-24/ty-article/.premium/algerias-first-kfc-restaurant-closes-amid-gaza-protests-reopens-without-logo/0000018f-1072-d70d-a58f-d9fbea650000

Zyglidopoulos, S., Georgiadis, A. P., Carroll, C. E., & Siegel, D. S. (2019). Does media attention drive corporate social responsibility? *Journal of Business Research*, 65(11), 1622–1627.

Index

Note: Page numbers followed by "n" denote endnotes.

For Product Safety Concerns and Information please contact our EU representative GPSR@taylorandfrancis.com
Taylor & Francis Verlag GmbH, Kaufingerstraße 24, 80331 München, Germany

www.ingramcontent.com/pod-product-compliance
Ingram Content Group UK Ltd.
Pitfield, Milton Keynes, MK11 3LW, UK
UKHW022109190926
475702UK00013B/1336
9780367616601